**Practising Destiny
Principles and Processes in Adult Learning**

Practising Destiny
Principles and Processes in Adult Learning

Coenraad van Houten

TEMPLE LODGE

Translated by J. Collis (and amended by the author)

Temple Lodge Publishing
Hillside House
The Square, Forest Row
East Sussex, RH18 5ES

www.templelodge.com

Published by Temple Lodge in association with New Adult Learning Movement 2000
Reprinted 2007

Originally published in German under the title *Erwachsenenbildung als Schicksalspraxis* by Verlag Freies Geistesleben, Stuttgart 1998

© Verlag Freies Geistesleben & Urachhaus GmbH 1998
This translation © Coenraad van Houten 2000

The moral right of the translator has been asserted under the Copyright, Designs and Patents Act, 1988

All rights reserved. No part of this publication may be reproduced, stored in a retrieval system, or transmitted, in any form or by any means, electronic, mechanical, photocopying, recording or otherwise, without the prior permission of the publishers

A catalogue record for this book is available from the British Library

ISBN 978 1902636 21 4

Cover by S. Gulbekian. Cover painting by Anne Stockton
Typeset by DP Photosetting, Aylesbury, Bucks.
Printed and bound by 4edge Limited, UK

Contents

Foreword 1

Introduction 5

Part One: What is Adult Learning?
1. The Three Learning Paths and Their Aims 13
2. The Adult Educator's Two Fundamental Principles and Seven Professional Fields 18
   The two fundamental principles 18
   The seven professional fields 21
   I. *Selflessly using the twelve senses* 22
   II. *Independently developing the three judgement processes* 24
       Learning to create an open space between observing (I) and judging (II) 30
   III. *The ability to encounter* 32
        Four preconditions 34
        The process of encounter 38
        The aim of encounter 39
   IV. *Mastering, distinguishing and integrating the three learning paths* 42
       Treading the three learning paths 42
       Distinguishing between the three learning paths 43
       Integrating the three learning paths 44
       The relationship between the ability to encounter (III) and the synthesis of the three learning paths (IV) 47
   V. *Day-time learning* 48
   VI. *Night-time learning* 50
       The bridge between day-time learning (V) and night-time learning (VI) 53

VII. Ability to manage the sevenfold learning process independently 58
Conclusion 60

Part Two: Destiny Learning

1. General Introduction to Destiny Learning 66

2. Destiny is the Reality in Which We Live 70
   Learning Step I 72
   1. *Observing a destiny event* 72
   2. *Collaboration in a group* 74
   3. *Hindrances to the learning process* 74
   4. *Helpful exercises* 75
   Learning Step II 76
   1. *Uniting the destiny event with one's biography* 76
   2. *Working together* 79
   3. *Supervising the learning process* 80
   4. *Overcoming the main blockages and hindrances* 81
   Learning Step III 81
   1. *Finding the causes and discovering the learning task they contain* 81
   2. *Finding the causes* 82
   3. *Discovering the learning task* 84
   4. *Working together* 84
   5. *Possible karmic causes in former lives* 87
   6. *The most intractable learning blockages* 90
   7. *Measures to protect the learning process* 95
   8. *Supportive activities for Learning Step III* 97
   Learning Step IV 98
   1. *Accepting one's destiny* 98
   2. *Working together in Step IV* 103
   3. *Some learning blockages* 104
   Learning Step V 105
   1. *Practising in daily life* 105
   2. *Preparation* 106
   3. *Day-time and night-time learning* 109

4. The dynamic between Learning Steps III,
   IV and V 110
5. Working together 114
6. Some learning blockages 115
Learning Step VI 119
1. Growing ability to observe the karmic web 119
2. How does this new gift come to expression? 120
3. How does the destiny sense develop? 121
4. Activities to support the development of the
   destiny sense 122
5. How to handle the destiny sense 122
Learning Step VII 123
1. Being creative in bringing order into destiny 123
2. Destiny actions that create order 123
3. Destiny actions as the source of a social art 124
4. Destiny actions as healing deeds 124
5. Destiny actions as a new conscience 125

3. Basic Attitude to Destiny 127

4. Summary and Conclusion 129

Part Three: The Adult Educator's Schooling Path

1. The Threefold Relationship Between Adult
   Educator and Participants 141
   1.1 Relating to one's own profession 141
   1.2 Creating a threefold relationship between adult
       educator and adult participant 142
       The relationship in Vocational Learning 143
       The relationship in Destiny Learning 146
       The relationship in Spiritual Research Learning 148
       Summary 152

2. Four Kinds of Time: Rhythm in Adult
   Education 154
   2.1 Clock time 154
   2.2 Living time or rhythm 155

    2.3 Psychological time 155
    2.4 Ego time 156

3. Self-Education of the Adult Educator 160

4. General Schooling of the Adult Educator 167

Part Four: Practical Applications

1. Human Encounter 171
   by *Shirley Routledge*

2. Judgement Forming—a Dynamic Model 177
   by *Lex Bos*

3. Some Exercises for Adult Learning and Destiny
   Learning 200
   by *C.J. van Houten*

4. The Seven Learning Steps in Painting Therapy ... 204
   by *Else Marie Henriksen*

5. Adult Learning in Teaching Speech Formation ... 206
   by *Enrica dal Zio*

6. Destiny Learning in Organizations 209
   by *Lauri Salonen*

7. How Biography Work Relates to Destiny
   Learning 217
   Karl Heinz Finke

Final Comment and Summary 222

Notes 227

Foreword

'As compared with children, how do adults learn?' This basic question provided the background to my first book, *Awakening the Will*.[1]

The present book also begins with a fundamental question: 'What capabilities does an adult human being need to school in order to lead a healthy life in the present age and environment and, over and above this, to give a creative contribution to the world?'

Many people experience the present time as threatening and destructive. They feel they are living in a world in which evil is not only visible but also on the increase. This book is intended to show that our age has a purpose that is hidden from us, the purpose of enabling humanity to take a new step in its evolution. Adult learning ought to serve this new evolutionary step, and it is hoped that the book will provide a contribution in that direction.

The author's earlier book, originally published in German, met with considerable interest in many countries, and it has found practical application in a number of educational establishments. It was, however, incomplete. Having explained some fundamental principles on which adult learning is based, among others that there are not one but three learning paths, it chiefly described only the first of these: Professional or Specialist Adult Learning, which we shall now call Vocational Learning. It sketched 'Destiny Learning' in outline only, and merely hinted at Spiritual Research Learning.

The need thus arose for a second and a third book in which the other two learning paths would be described in as much detail as the first. This made it necessary to gather a great deal of practical experience through a kind of research based on experiment and discovery in which the most essential contributions would come from the adult participants and colleagues in many seminars.

So we set out to design, implement and evaluate seminars on Destiny Learning and on Spiritual Research Learning. One main contribution came from the nine-week 'Anthroposophical Schooling Course' held at the former Centre for Social Development in Sussex, England. For many years this centre developed the three learning paths as a new form of adult learning. These three learning paths have also been worked through at the Forum Kreuzberg in Berlin, once in a nine-day and once in a three-week seminar. The three learning paths have also been presented in sequence during a twelve-day seminar in Weimar, Germany. They are now beginning to appear integrated into the manner in which adult education is being practised.

All this led to two important discoveries:

1. The three learning paths constitute an organic whole in the way they mutually reinforce, complement and supplement one another. They also qualify one another, as we shall see.
2. Together the three learning paths create a fourth element that could become the source of a future form of adult learning. This element arises through the way the combination of the three paths enables all aspects of the human being to be addressed and also to express itself.

These discoveries, repeatedly confirmed by course participants, make it necessary to deepen and redefine what has already been worked through in the realm of adult learning. Part I of this book will deal with this in detail. Regarding the situation in educational establishments it becomes obvious that the tasks and schooling of future adult educators will need to be both enhanced and expanded. Part Two is devoted to Destiny Learning. (A third book, still to be written, will concern itself with learning for Spiritual Research.) Part Three, 'The Adult Educator's Schooling Path', suggests what a future schooling for adult educators might look like. Part Four contains a collection of specific applications, experiences and exercises developed by the adult educators who are already broadening and deepening the new adult education.

I have yielded to increasing pressure from course participants and others to get this book written as quickly as possible. Consequently, as with the first book, I feel very strongly that all this is only a beginning which will need improvement and further development before it can be written about as a finished product.

Perhaps this feeling is an ingredient of the new profession of adult educator, for anything inadequate or unfinished invites us to work on improvements and further developments. In this sense the book is intended as an invitation and not a final answer to a new adult education.

An author must never forget those to whom he owes what he has written down. In this case the list is tremendously long. It comprises all the participants in many seminars and courses; also the many colleagues who meanwhile constitute an international group and who have tried out new forms of teaching, often with considerable uncertainty and risk; furthermore private individuals and educational establishments who have dared to offer new and unusual seminars in many countries: Germany (the majority), England, Finland, Sweden, Holland, Canada, the USA, South Africa, New Zealand, Australia and various other countries.

Again and again it has proved true that adult learning, as indeed any learning, should be a preparation for the future. If we prepare ourselves now to be adult educators, perhaps we shall succeed in meeting the events and demands of the twenty-first century in a creative way that will enable us to find the right answers. This will be the task of the adult education profession in the future.

One final remark: This book has been written primarily for *adult educators*—as a contribution towards a renewal of adult learning befitting modern times. Yet this adult learning is not yet practised everywhere. It is conceivable that when these fundamental principles, learning processes and methods are one day applied on a broad base, the institutionalized forms of adult learning will have to change and might partly disappear, and that actual learning and development processes will take place as part of everyday life and everyday work. Therefore this book is also written for all those who want to become independent *adult learners* following their own personal path!

Coenraad van Houten
Forest Row, England

Introduction

Education for adults should provide answers to the difficulties, challenges and questions posed by today's economic, political, social, cultural and spiritual situation, a situation much changed since the beginning of the twentieth century and likely to continue changing at great speed if only because of the ongoing rapid development of technology, not least information technology.

All over the world in varying degrees technology and economics are more and more coming to dominate daily life. Adult education will therefore have to foster entirely new capabilities to cope with these changes in the world and in life situations. In former times a good basic education, with mostly a vocational or academic training added, was all we required in order to find our own way in life. Not so today. We now need to school quite specific new faculties in ourselves to be able to meet present life situations in a creative way.

A thorough investigation into how the individual human being is determined, conditioned, even blocked, by the pressures and demands of daily living, as well as postgraduate educational systems, will reveal which dormant human faculties are being neglected, conditioned or even suffocated with a specific purposefulness, faculties that will be sorely needed if we are to withstand the pressures as well as find creative answers to them. These faculties—of which the basic ones will be dealt with in the following pages—remain dormant if not consciously nurtured and developed by the independent adult ego through an adult education that can truly meet the challenges of our time. A good school education up to 21 years is a necessary preparation in that it unfolds the child's abilities, but it is not enough for today's challenges.

Here are a few examples: The countries of Europe were totally unprepared for what National Socialism could do to people. The way in which life under a Communist system could condition a people is still scarcely understood. Vaclav Havel and many others have given us vivid descriptions of the inner strengths required if one wanted to remain human under such systems. Both these political models can be expected to return—albeit under different names and with different faces. Will we be prepared when this happens?

Another model of global proportions is that of an economic, technical, commercial determinism which demands that economic prosperity must have priority over everything else. It is a philosophy emanating from the West that has gradually been taken over by the rest of the world, and all education, certainly adult education, will be expected to serve it at all costs, thus placing human needs under the dictatorship of economic necessity. Perhaps this appears exaggerated, yet the creeping trend of increasingly materialistic values can be detected everywhere. It is a trend—relatively unnoticed as yet—which causes economic and technological requirements to gain increasing control over the behaviour of human beings by getting them to adjust to and fit in with a global economic system. This may seem logical, but it is not human when given priority over all other values in life. What better control than by means of a vocational training that is determined by economic principles and aims and has to abide by certain worldwide rules? If this succeeds, humanity will have a techno-economic and material future, but not a human future.

Many other conditioning trends can be detected as well. The above are merely a few indications.

It is hoped that the descriptions in, Part One of the Seven Professional Fields and the Two Fundamental Principles will be perceived in this sense; and the same applies to what Parts Two and Three have to say about Destiny Learning and the schooling of the adult educator. Healthy adult learning, which schools and strengthens genuine human capacities and the individual's creativity and ability to develop, will enable people to stand up to the world in a constructive way. It teaches us to regard today's life and culture as an area that

Introduction 7

challenges us to seek new developments, thus lending meaning to today's worldwide problems: they become the arena where a new step in human evolution can be practised. We thus learn to discern that it is humanity's problems which show us what ought to be developed. The signs of the times are our teachers! Each of us must find and school the answers independently, while the adult educator's task is to make this possible, provide the means and show the learning paths.

*

At this juncture let us take a brief look at the content of the book *Awakening the Will*, since the content of the present book will be based on the foundations laid there.[2]

Its title states its main objective, which is to find ways of enabling adult human beings to apply their will independently in future, without any external stimulus, pressure, discipline or alien determination. On the surface this may appear to be a question of action, but at its root it refers to the way adults can and do learn. We all know that even education itself is nowadays strongly influenced by our technological age and its presuppositions. Various superimposed systems have paralysed and shackled the independent will to learn, which is bound up with the will to change and the will to develop. The book therefore states that the profession of adult educator will have to acquire an entirely new profile, which can be achieved by building on three fundamental impulses that lie dormant in every human being and need to be aroused: the impulse for understanding, the impulse for development, and the impulse for improvement or seeking to do things better. It will be the task of a future adult education to awaken these, and this will be possible if the learning process itself can be individualized in all the fields—manual, intellectual, artistic and scientific—in which learning takes place.

Awakening the Will also shows that the adult learning process is supported by the seven life processes which are responsible for the proper functioning of our bodily organization: 1. breathing, 2. warming, 3. nourishing, 4. secreting (sorting), 5. maintaining, 6. growing, 7. reproducing.

When these seven life processes of the body are transformed by the ego into the seven learning processes of adult learning, a spiritual organism arises in the human being that is more independent of the physical body. One way of expressing this would be to say that the seven life processes take care of the biological part of the human being; then, by transforming these into individual activities through the learning process, the ego develops the spiritual, cultural part of the human being.

Between the fifth and seventh year of life a portion of the life processes ceases to be needed for maintenance of the bodily organization and is therefore placed at the disposal of the learning processes. Initially these are cared for and developed through up-bringing and education. After the age of 21, however, the conscious ego should learn to master the learning processes independently, and this is where adult education begins.

The learning processes that arise out of the transformed

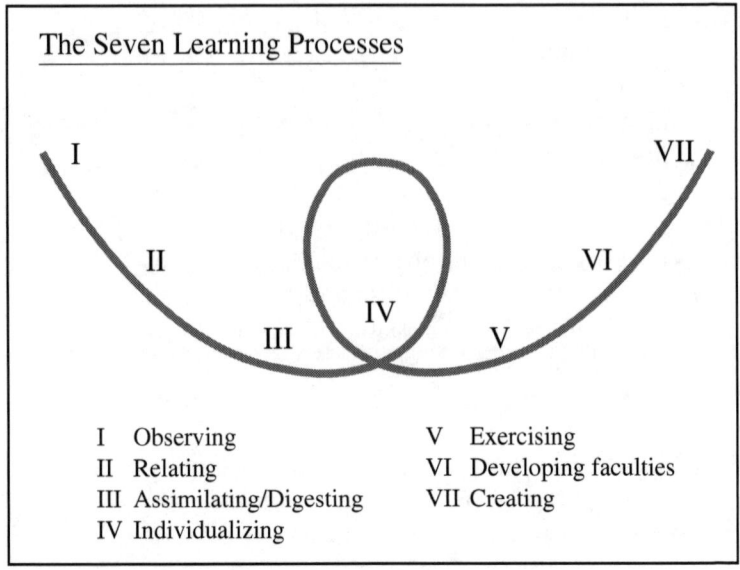

Diagram 1

life processes are: 1. observing, 2. relating, 3. assimilating/ digesting, 4. individualizing, 5. exercising, 6. developing new faculties, 7. creating. (See Diagram 1.)
The first four steps form a unit in some respects. They are more knowledge-oriented and lead from the outside inwards. Something new—individualizing—arises at the fourth step, which forms a starting point for the last three. These lead from the inside outwards and are primarily will-oriented.

By setting current training programmes against these seven steps it is easy to discover where these learning processes are either entirely absent or barely present. This will point to the degree to which a training programme aims to produce conditioned individuals who readily toe the line, or to provide the type of adult learning that fits the aims formulated above.

Awakening the Will shows the foundations on which adults can 'learn how to learn'. The present book goes more deeply and broadly into these foundations, the focus being on Destiny Learning. Finally, in a further book the learning path of Spiritual or Creative Research will be worked out in greater detail.

Part One:
What is Adult Learning?

1. The Three Learning Paths and Their Aims

Although this book deals primarily with the second learning path, Destiny Learning, it seems appropriate to provide an overview of all three learning paths for the better orientation of the reader.

*

The first path comprises all the learning we need in order to cope with our working life. This includes all kinds of specialist training but also everything we need in order to hold our own in an increasingly technological world. In a nutshell it is everything we can learn at universities, colleges, training colleges, evening classes and so on. Since science and its applications are developing rapidly, and since the psychological configuration of the human being is also changing fast, we have to assume that the need for this learning will increase. The question is how we shall manage to keep up with this need in the future. We shall use the term *Vocational Learning* to denote one basic path in this direction. It provides the foundation for the other two learning paths and depends on our ability to use our independent ego to transform the seven life processes in our organism into seven conscious learning processes. The seven processes form an organic whole and must be fully mastered if Vocational Learning is to take place properly.

*

The second path rests on the understanding that studying our biography reveals another learning process, one that can lead to a form of 'learning through life'. Life confronts us with learning situations; by mastering these we further our own personal development. These learning situations are destiny situations. We can be led to very profound self-knowledge through the way destiny unfolds. We can learn *for* life, but also *through* life. The second learning path has therefore been termed *Destiny Learning*.

Destiny Learning is a conscious path of learning in which our awareness must continue to increase. It too, therefore, rests on the transformation of the seven life processes by our ego. Its aim, however, is different, for the aim of Destiny Learning is self-knowledge. The subject matter to be studied is also different, for it is destiny itself, or 'karma' in its ancient Indian designation. The seven steps also therefore have different names and come to expression as a further development of those in Vocational Learning. Destiny Learning, too, aims for the development of new capabilities. The main emphasis in this process is on developing the perception of destiny (Learning Step VI), so that we can approach our destiny creatively and bring order into it (Learning Step VII).

This is not intended as any form of therapy or help in a life crisis. It is a learning process that schools adults to become ever better at bringing about their own Destiny Learning. The seven Learning Steps are described in detail in Part Two and are therefore merely listed in Diagram 2 so that (reading from left to right) they can be compared with the two other learning paths.

*

In *Awakening the Will*[1] the third learning path came to be termed the Spiritual Schooling Path because historically spiritual schooling, or the schooling of senses for spiritual perception, was the original, most ancient form of learning. All learning was brought into human history by the ancient Mystery Schools. In contrast to those early times, if this path is to be trodden in a manner that befits our present age it must be an entirely independent and individual path of knowledge in which the individual student remains solely responsible for every step taken. The schooling path thus becomes a path of knowledge and understanding. When this path of knowledge becomes real in our daily life, in our working life and indeed in our whole attitude in life, in other words when it is applied and practised, it is given the modern designation *spiritual research*.

The manner in which scientific research is conducted has taken on an entirely new character in modern times. The same basic attitude involved is also applied in spiritual

The Three Learning Paths and Their Aims   15

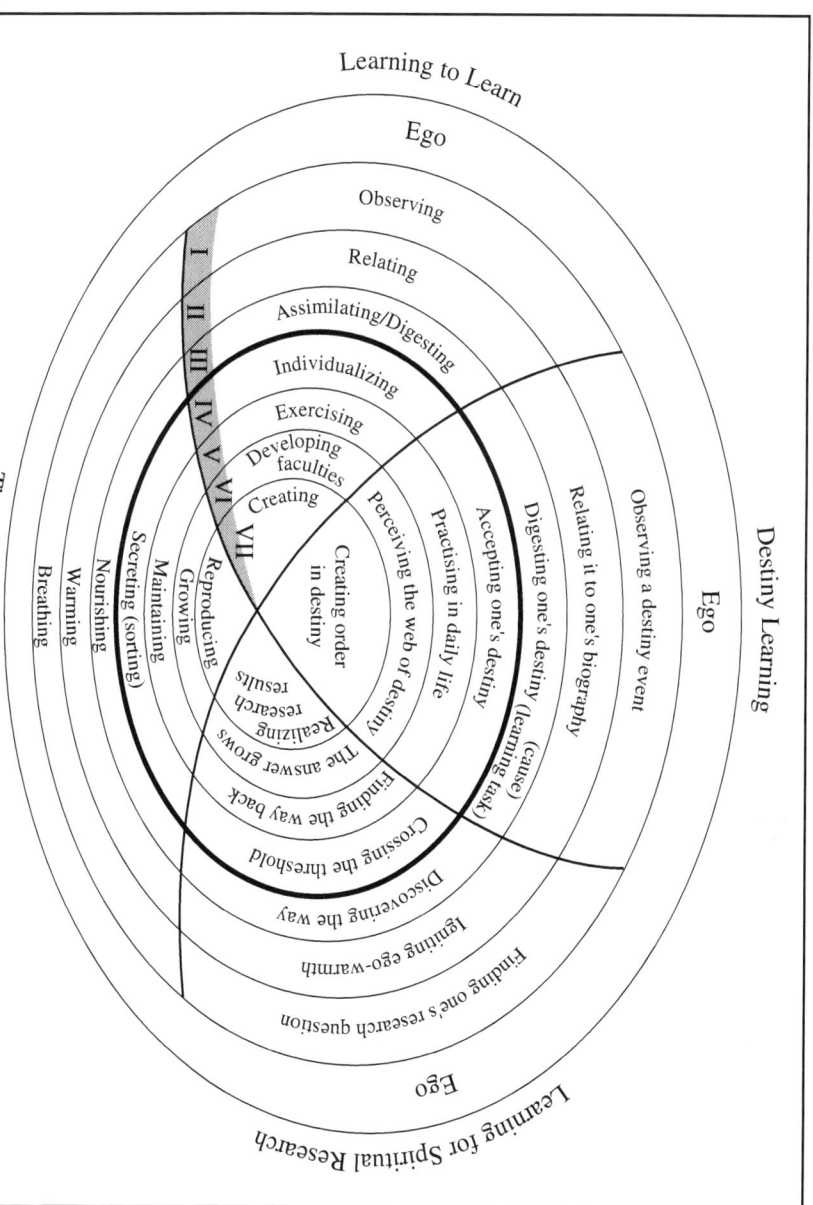

Diagram 2

research, only here the methods and aims are different. The differences and similarities will be discussed further when the third book is written. Spiritual research can be learnt, so the third learning path might also be termed *Spiritual Research Learning*. Once again its roots may be found in the seven life processes. The learning steps, though, are essentially different in the way they arise from the type of research and its aims. Comparing the three paths horizontally we find that Spiritual Research Learning requires the greatest intensification of the seven learning processes and that it is a further refinement of the other two learning paths. This is not surprising when one considers that both scientific and spiritual research have the task of bringing new elements into our culture, thus shaping the future.

*

The question remains as to whether Spiritual Research Learning needs to be preceded by the other two paths of adult learning, and it is to be hoped that by the end of this book readers will have found their own answer. Let it be said already, though, that in principle Spiritual Research Learning is possible for everybody, although to a different degree. Spiritual research is not the sole prerogative of highly-developed initiates or leaders of humanity; every individual can, and indeed should, strive to achieve it, for it is a requirement of our age, as mentioned in the introduction where reference is made to the need to provide creative answers to the challenges of our time.

One of the main signs of this is the fact that today's exceedingly specialized training often leads to considerable professional deformation in later life. The reason for this is that people have never learnt to question themselves and have not been taught from the outset how to adopt a basic research attitude that can lead to continuous renewal of their own profession.

When one contemplates the three times seven steps shown in Diagram 2 one by one, then studies the vertically depicted learning processes carefully in their horizontal relationship with one another as an intensifying continuum, and finally experiences the three 'individualizations' (Individualizing,

The Three Learning Paths and Their Aims 17

Accepting one's destiny, Crossing the threshold) as the core of the learning process for adults, then one will gain an inkling of how all three together form a totality that addresses the learning human being also as a totality. Who in the depths of his being doesn't want to make continual improvements in his working life (Vocational Learning), thereby getting to know himself ever more profoundly (Destiny Learning) and finally join others creatively in shaping the future (Spiritual Research Learning)! The attempt will be made in the following chapters to clarify this as thoroughly as possible.

2. The Adult Educator's Two Fundamental Principles and Seven Professional Fields

The two fundamental principles

The ongoing awakening of the adult learner's *will to learn* is the main aim of Vocational Learning. It is in fact a main element in all three learning paths, and needs to be enhanced even further for Destiny Learning and Spiritual Research Learning.

The second fundamental principle—which constitutes a polarity with the first—that must be unceasingly generated is the *sense of truth*, a feeling for the truth. The *will to learn* can be kindled; but a sense, and especially the *sense of truth*, is not experienced until it comes to expression by being used. It is important to *distinguish* between the way illusions, constructs and such things manifest and the way the sense of truth comes to expression, for we only gradually learn to trust that our sense of truth will indeed lead us to a reality that is true. The moment we begin to think about it, it disappears, and our intellect starts to play tricks on us again, making us doubt everything.

With Vocational Learning, emphasis was on the will to learn, which is based chiefly on awakening the three impulses that lie dormant in us—the impulse for knowing, the impulse for development, and the impulse for improvement or perfection. By contrast, in Destiny Learning, which has to do with self-knowledge, and even more in Spiritual Research Learning, it is the sense of truth that is far more deeply addressed and called upon. When this does not happen it is easy to lose oneself because one is much less likely to be corrected by earthly reality than is the case in Vocational Learning.

An adult educator wanting to bring the three learning

The Adult Educator's Two Fundamental Principles

paths into his professional work therefore faces two main tasks that should mesh with his work in all kinds of ways: *awakening the will to learn* and *developing the sense of truth*.

*

Straightforward observation tells us that a sense of truth exists, for without it any search for knowledge would be meaningless. Various other languages confirm that we are talking about a *sense*: Sinn für Wahrheit, waarheids zin (gevoel), sense de vérité, etc. As with all other senses, this sense needs to be educated, schooled and used if it is to fulfil its function. Awakening the will to learn and generating the sense of truth are thus lodestar and compass for the adult educator in all his work. (See Diagram 3, p. 21.)

Clearly the sense of truth deserves a far more thorough investigation, but for our present purposes we shall observe its application in practical situations since it penetrates all seven professional fields of the adult educator. We shall also mention it in the section on the three judgement processes (II below), and can therefore desist from further discussion here.

The following simplified exercise is suggested as a way of demonstrating how far the decadence of today's culture has already progressed with regard to our awareness of the truth:

1. Spend a short period of perhaps an hour thoroughly inspecting the information you are presented with, e.g. in the newspaper, during a walk, via the junk mail in your letterbox, on TV and radio, in the supermarket, during a conversation, and so on.
2. Then confront this information with the question: Is all this actually true?
3. You discover that very little of it is accurate. All this superfluous, obtrusive information bombarding our senses has a very strong, unremitting influence on us, especially in the way it counteracts our feeling for the truth by bringing about a short circuit between the sense impression and our urges, hidden desires, fears and so on. Yet no one protests against this daily bombardment of untruths. Why not? Has our feeling for the truth gone fast asleep?

An exercise like this demonstrates clearly that the second fundamental principle of all adult learning—the first being the will to learn—ought long since to have been addressed much more strongly in our culture to prevent its loss and an accompanying ongoing advance of cultural decadence. Untruth is today a cultural phenomenon that is accepted without much criticism.

In consequence of these developments the sense of truth is questioned; indeed its very existence is denied. The fact is that if the sense of truth is neither schooled nor noticed it ceases to exist!

There is a second exercise that would benefit us all and most certainly the adult educator:

1. Think back to a moment in your life when you had an experience of truth, a feeling of certainty that said to you: 'This is true, this is right, this would be a good thing!' Your intellect will be quick to cast doubt on this and bring a return to confusion. Yet you can feel certain that this experience did happen and did last for a few short seconds. Our primeval trust in the reliability of our thinking and the activity of forming judgements needs to be reaffirmed by such exercises, otherwise any adult learning will be pointless. We can only recognize the sense of truth by using it.
2. This exercise can show us that a sense of truth is indeed dormant in us and that it can be strengthened through constant practice.

So how can the sense of truth be schooled and the will to learn be awakened? It can be done if the independent adult learner or the adult educator methodically develops and works out the seven professional fields described in the next section. These should provide the instruments needed for the continuous care of the two fundamental principles. It will be noticed that the two fundamental principles of the *will to learn* and the *sense of truth* mutually complement, strengthen and confirm one another. (See Diagram 3.)

The Adult Educator's Two Fundamental Principles

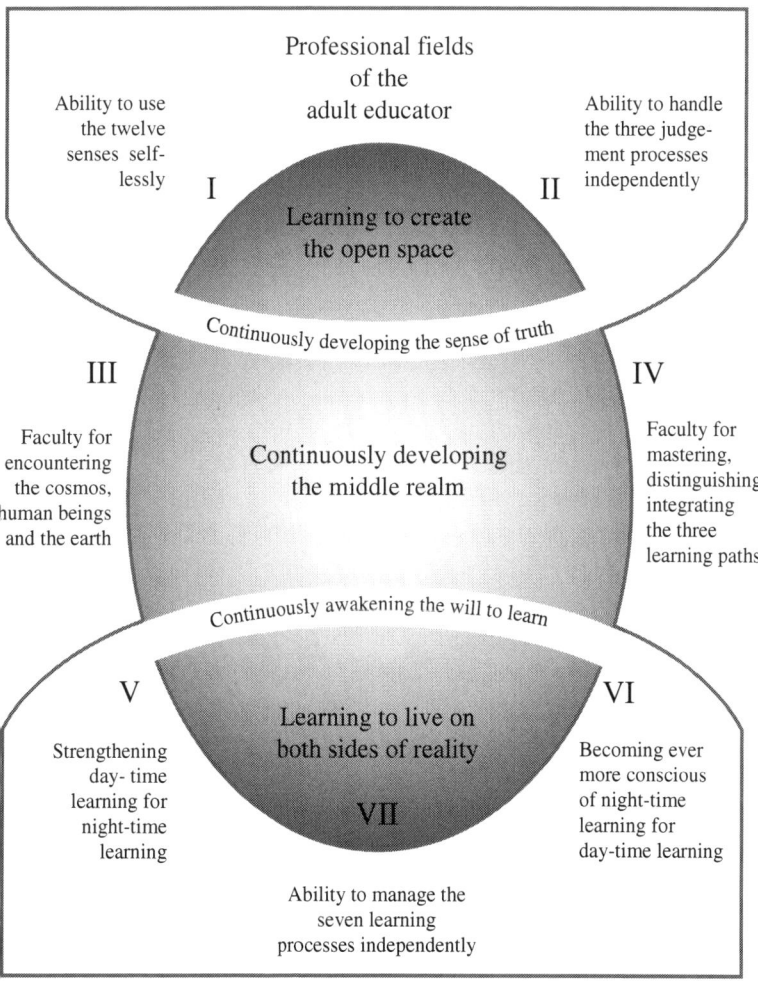

Diagram 3

The seven professional fields

The following sections will discuss sensory observation (I) and judgement forming (II). *Judgement forming* is the process of searching that takes place between observing and thinking. (The word 'judgement' is used here in this sense, not as assessment of 'right' or 'wrong'.) *Sensory observation* denotes the use of the twelve senses as described in spiritual science. One of these senses is the sense of thought by which concepts and ideas are observed. *Thinking* as such refers to the force by means of which we can distinguish between concepts, ideas and mental pictures while also seeing what connects them.

I. Selflessly using the twelve senses

Nowadays objective, factual observation is becoming increasingly threatened. In our present civilization the unsuspecting observer is bombarded with sensory stimuli to such a degree that initially he cannot help succumbing to the influence of these external stimuli. By contrast, a reflective, conscientious, accurate observation of objects can only take place if one not only makes an effort but also does so regularly—which is the same as kindling the will to learn by using one's senses properly. Observing is a learning activity of the ego which involves the ego exercising restraint during the period of observation. If it does not do this, one merely sees oneself reflected by the external world, and this is indeed a frequent occurrence. So it is necessary to school a sensory activity that is as selfless as possible.

This refers to all twelve senses including the more spiritual ones such as the sense of language, the sense that discerns thinking, and the ego sense. Our muscles atrophy if we do not use them regularly, and the same happens to our twelve senses if we do not use them in the right way, i.e. objectively. We only discover how little we use these twelve windows on the world in a way that avoids anything personal or subjective once we have developed the will to learn and begin to practise 'selfless' observation.

Since our feeling for the truth is founded on the firm ground of sense perception, the capacity to observe is the footing upon which any adult learning must stand.

Because we possess twelve senses, schooling our capacity to observe is a highly differentiated process, as well as being one that progresses through various stages. And since we have twelve senses, each of which shows a different quality, this process also schools our power of discernment. If we possessed only a single sense this would be impossible. Here are the twelve senses:

Sense of touch	Sense of smell	Sense of hearing
Sense of life	Sense of taste	Sense of language
Sense of movement	Sense of sight	Sense of thought
Sense of balance	Sense of warmth	Sense of ego

Adult educators who practised using their senses soon noticed that regular exercise of sensory activity rapidly increased their capacity for learning. Learning processes accompanied daily by short exercises in observation soon proved very effective. Capacities such as restraint, openness, wonder and concentration should be practised constantly, for all learning is mediated by the senses. The better the senses function, the better will the learning be. Therefore the capacity to observe is the foundation on which adult learning should stand.

Schooling this capacity also provides the basis for developing one's feeling for the truth. So long as one cannot distinguish clearly between objective observation and the influence of one's own being on the perception, one's feeling for the truth will remain insecure. It will become more accurate to the same degree that such distinction succeeds.

An even higher learning aim also lives in this professional field, for selfless use of the senses is only the first step. What comes to be revealed through the senses can deepen, step by step, into a view of the essence of things observed. This way of observing phenomena was initiated by Goethe and followed by others, but applied mainly to the world of nature. It now needs to be extended to encompass all realms of life.

Selfless observation of our fellow human beings can also lead to the ability to see their true being, something that will become decisively significant in all professions that have to do directly with people. Although schooling the senses can be a specialized subject to be taught, it is included here as one of the professional fields of the adult educator because observation through the senses takes place constantly in Vocational Learning. It is also a schooling through which we can observe our own inner world in the same selfless fashion, and this is of great importance for our self-knowledge in Destiny Learning. Furthermore, Spiritual Research Learning requires us to be alert witnesses of supersensible phenomena so that we can assess them correctly. With regard to supersensible perceptions, the capacity to observe must therefore be further enhanced.

Perhaps we should add that totally selfless sensory observation can never be entirely attained, and for this very reason one must continue to strive for it. To observe the world totally selflessly would mean losing oneself entirely and dissolving into the universe. The process whereby the ego is fully present and actively penetrates the senses protects us against this.

II. Independently developing the three judgement processes
Independently forming judgements is the adult educator's second development and professional field. It is directly related to the selfless use of the senses. In this case, too, it is easy to tell how our ability to form judgements becomes less independent if we do not constantly school it. We form judgements all day long, but how often are these judgements in fact merely second-hand, induced, conditioned or automatic 'pre-judgements', i.e. prejudices? Where and when is a judgement formed independently as a conscious, original deed? We all know the extent to which public opinion is manipulated and how consumers are seduced to buy things they do not need. The trouble in this age of information overload and manipulation is that we are insufficiently aware either of how little independent judgement forming activity we engage in or how strongly our thinking is determined by outside influences.

In his book *Antipolitik*, György Konrad stated that the future will be determined primarily by a small elite group of 'independent thinkers' who can be found in all walks of life.[2] They do not necessarily share the same opinion, but they

The Adult Educator's Two Fundamental Principles 25

have great respect for one another because they have not abandoned the creative gift of the human spirit to form independent judgements.

The very fact that human beings do not as a matter of course possess the ability to form independent judgements makes it essential for us to cultivate and practise this ability constantly in all forms of adult learning. This also leads to the awakening of a feeling for the truth. The concept of 'forming judgements' must not, however, be interpreted too narrowly, for it takes place not only cognitively but also aesthetically and morally (as already mentioned in *Awakening the Will*).

The professional field of judgement formation encompasses all three judgement processes, and they combine to develop the sense of truth. Each process works in a different way, has its own laws and supports and qualifies the others. The creative element, for example, is chiefly addressed by the formation of aesthetic judgement, which is why this type of judgement does most to strengthen independence. If one is serious about developing the capacity to form judgements *independently*, it is not enough to school only the cognitive aspect, for independence requires particularly the capacity to form aesthetic judgements also. So all three types of judgement formation must be schooled together. It is hoped that this fundamental principle will become clearer as we proceed.

Forming a *cognitive judgement* involves a process of getting to know, understand and recognize the essential nature of an object, of whatever kind. This object can be either an inner or an outer *experience*. Anything subjective disturbs and distorts this process, and must therefore be put aside. We are concerned solely with persuading the object itself to reveal what it is really like.

Forming an *aesthetic judgement* involves *encountering* the object (as opposed to merely recognizing or perceiving it). In the confrontation between human beings and their environment, judgements arise that express something of this encounter. An encounter always takes place between two entities who both have the right to exist. The best judgements are those that express as truthfully as possible the balance between and the significance of both.

Language is an example of a continuous process of forming aesthetic judgements. In fact it is a primary phenomenon in the way it builds a bridge between inner and outer and expresses the essential nature of both. Every choice of a word involves countless judgements. Behind every choice of words and every mode of expression lurks the question: Does what is being said give expression more to the speaker or to the matter in hand, or does it perhaps express both equally?

The process of aesthetic judgement forming could also be termed the process of relationships or of relational judgements since it always expresses the relationship between a human being and something in his environment. In this sense the formation of *social judgements* is identical with that of forming aesthetic judgements. If we do not school ourselves in forming social judgements, we nevertheless continuously form such judgements semi-consciously or automatically, the result being off-balance. In consequence the encounter aspect is very often eradicated.

Cognitive judgement forming is of course an important prerequisite and support for aesthetic judgement forming, since cognitive judgements are also necessary for an encounter between one person and another. Nevertheless, if one of the two possesses only cognitive judgements, then the personal encounter becomes fairly impossible.

In summary: The process of forming aesthetic judgements differs fundamentally from that of cognitive judgement formation, for in the latter case one's concern is directed exclusively towards the thought or object being investigated and not at all towards oneself. In the case of aesthetic judgements one is concerned with oneself and with the object; the two encounter one another in the judgement process, and we are concerned with the true relationship between the two. (See Diagram 4.)

Forming a *moral judgement* is the opposite of forming a cognitive one because in a moral judgement one is the central actor having to reach a moral decision in a specific life

The Adult Educator's Two Fundamental Principles 27

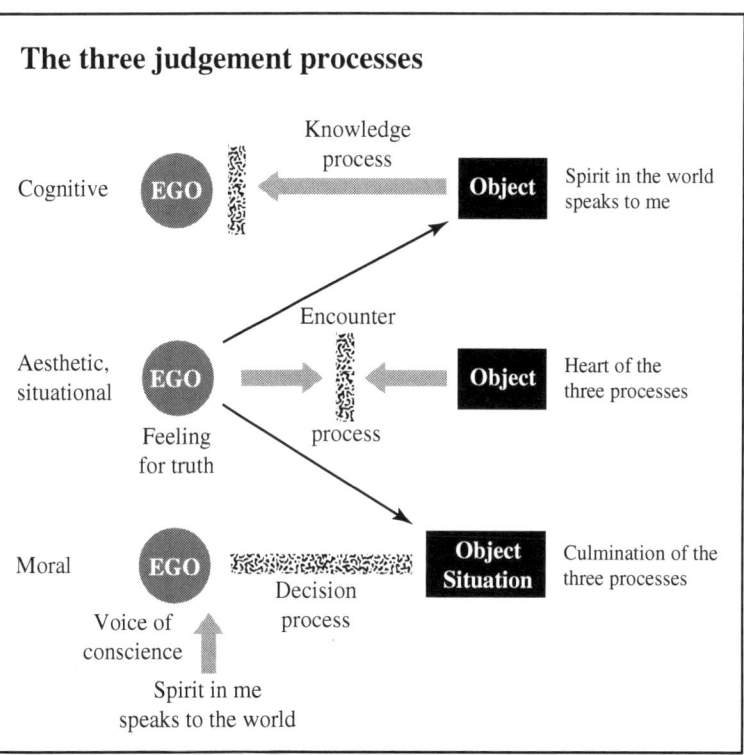

Diagram 4

situation. The first type of judgement formation is a cognitive process, the second an encounter event, and the third a form of decision-making. One's own moral responsibility is called for. In the first type of judgement the object reveals its essential nature; in the third, one must listen inwardly to the voice of one's own conscience. We are not used to this.

That is why the process of forming a moral judgement is so often smothered by cognitive processes that make one try to derive the moral law from the external situation instead of seeking it within oneself. Our ability to form moral judgements is often feeble precisely because the experience of listening to one's inner voice scarcely takes place at all. Nevertheless, it often turns out that moral understanding, though dormant, is indeed present and has the capacity for development. But for this to happen it must be schooled.

Assuming that in any situation moral action must be a new creative deed of freedom, it goes without saying that forming a moral judgement is the culmination of the three processes, since an act that is morally fruitful and meaningful requires a correct understanding of the situation, a creative and original form of encounter, and a decision founded on one's own free moral judgement. In this sense schooling the first two types of judgement becomes the precondition for forming moral judgements. In every independent cognitive judgement we awaken the human spirit; in every encounter we exercise this spirit. Every encounter also carries a truth within it. It brings the sense of truth into action so that it can be schooled. Then, in the moral decision taken at the decisive moment, the human spirit can appear as an awakening of the will and as a presence of mind and spirit. This shows what it means for the adult educator to develop this area and let the learning process become part of it, for the future depends on our deeds.

If one lives for a long time with the question as to what it is that the schooling paths of the three types of judgement actually bring about in us, then it can dawn on one that cognitive judgement and moral judgement come from the same source. On the path of knowledge the world spirit reveals itself to the human spirit from outside; in a truly moral decision the world spirit speaks to the human spirit from within and is individually experienced. The spirit of conscience contains both spirit and knowledge; in it the fundamental principles of awakening the will and the sense of truth are united. To bring forth the first dawn of this feeling of freedom can become a guiding image for the adult educator so that right from the start the adult learner can have the experience: 'I myself can find the answers to my questions; I can test the truth of whatever is stated; I can be responsible for my own actions.'

This professional field does not end with the schooling of the three types of judgement forming. It requires in addition that independence and individualization be continuously strengthened through such schooling.

Not only must moral judgement forming be developed as the 'culmination' of the three, but aesthetic judgement forming must become the 'heart' of the three. From this point of view, aesthetic—or situational and social—judgement is based on the following:

1. There needs to be an unceasing development, differentiation and refinement of our judging feeling life on the one hand and a constant enlivening of our sense impressions on the other.
2. When these two come together the situational judgement is born.
3. The better the balance between the two processes, the better the judgement.
4. Whenever there is artistic and social activity, which means whenever a judgement is *applied*, a new situation arises. From this arises a continuous process that is creative—a creative process of judging. This creativity is the source of independence. As the adult educator can come to realize, this is where the origin of independent judgement is found which can lend buoyancy to the other two kinds of judgement. Our feeling which has been schooled and ennobled through aesthetic activity can rise in the realm of cognition to become the feeling for truth in logical thinking; and can descend into moral judgement, sensing its way inwards where it can become a listening to the voice of conscience. Thus all our judging arises in the midst of our soul, in our life of feeling, and goes on to develop in cognition, in encounter, and in action.

These facts become even more impressive when we consider that a whole value system lies hidden, more or less dormant, in our feelings. After all, we evaluate the whole world in accordance with our feelings. By schooling the three processes of judging we bring this evaluation more and more into consciousness and can reshape it. As we shall see, Destiny Learning (Part Two) is the realm where we are concerned with these processes in a particular sense, for here we endeavour to develop a clear understanding of our own being.

Friedrich Schiller called this productive, aesthetic judgement forming the 'play impulse': 'The human being only becomes truly human when he is playing.'[3] Today in adult learning the play impulse must become the mainspring of independent judgement forming. 'Everything still remains to be done,' said Goethe. It is astonishing how much of what the German Idealists managed to work out is now so urgently demanded by our age. The ideas often exist already, but practical realization of these ideas is rare.

The purpose of describing the threefold judgement process here was to show the adult educator that the faculty of forming independent judgements needs to be schooled by every adult. However, the intention was not to describe the one and only route to this end but, on the contrary, rather to encourage others to discover many other patterns and resulting paths that can also lead to the aim of 'independent judgement forming'.

Learning to create an open space between observing (I) and judging (II)

No more explanation is needed as to why sensory observation and judgement forming are intimately linked, for they are both fundamental elements in all our understanding of knowledge. However, if they intermingle merely automatically or instinctively, then observation is not selfless and judgement forming not independent. The most endangered in this respect is aesthetic judgement forming for it is at present the weakest and most delicate of the three types of judgement formation.

Our sensory activity—and with it our capacity for genuine encounter—is attacked from outside by media such as advertising, videos, TV, radio and films. Our feeling life protects itself against these things by shutting itself off from them. This easily leads to the blunting of our senses so that they then need ever greater stimuli to function, and in many cases this results in a vicious circle that can lead to addictions.

The Adult Educator's Two Fundamental Principles

Our life of feeling—and with it once again our capacity for genuine encounter—is also attacked, but from within, by everything that arises from our unconscious by way of fear, anger, hate and so on. These feelings are either suppressed or acted out, but in either case little is done to work them through and transform them.

These attacks on the central core of the human being work against our ability to send out feelers both inwards and outwards and therefore also against pure sensory observation. They also work against the independent cultivation of judgement formation, especially in its aesthetic aspects.

What can we use as our guiding image to counter this?

The attacks in both these areas call for our inner activity, the activity of our ego to create an open space, a platform where we ourselves can on the one hand selflessly observe and on the other guide our own judgement processes. This 'creation of an open space' is increasingly enhanced by schooling the senses and by active judgement formation (as already mentioned in the previous section). Without this 'open space', which we generate ourselves, we are totally lost as regards any independence. This is why all adult learning necessitates the development of both these professional fields, so that something new can arise out of their inter-relationship. This new element is the feeling or sense for truth. Common sense takes on a deeper meaning! Learning how to create the open space is one of the core themes in connection with adult learning. It will therefore reappear in the coming sections from various further points of view.

One way of looking at our sense of truth would be to regard it as a synthesis of the twelve senses—a thirteenth sense which arises when we use the other twelve in a selfless way and which is nourished by the three types of judgement forming. This enhances our experience of the universal character of our thought world. Our thinking is founded on our sense of thought, which is our faculty of being able to observe thoughts. It moves about between countless concepts, ideas and inner pictures, constantly endeavouring to unite these with one another in ways that will yield a meaningful totality. Experiencing this universal totality of the thought world provides nourishment for our feeling for the truth. Through pure sensory activity this feeling for the truth is developed until it becomes the power of objective discrimination (Goethe's *'anschauende Urteilskraft'*) and is enhanced by the thought activity of forming concepts.

A very great deal depends for the future not only on whether all adult learning can plant the seeds of our feeling for the truth but also on whether it can then continuously nourish and develop it further. As we shall see, it is vital for the attainment of this aim that the two other learning paths—Destiny Learning and Spiritual Research Learning—should be added to the path of Vocational Learning.[4]

III. The ability to encounter

In social life today coping with relationships appears to be growing ever more difficult, and this applies both to the macrosocial realm with its many complicated and apparently insoluble conflicts and to the microsocial scene in which people are finding it increasingly difficult to form permanent relationships. Some people who have worked or lived together for years find themselves admitting that they have never really got to know one another. The other person remains an enigma; something in the way he or she behaves is somehow incomprehensible. This problem of alienation needs no further description here since it is frequently discussed in detail elsewhere. The fact that this internal abyss between individuals, groups and nations is growing deeper is a sure sign of the need to develop new faculties for bringing about real encounters.

The counter-images appearing in our civilization often demonstrate what adult learning is all about. One such counter-image of human encounter is torture and the accompanying interrogation. Torture is used as a means of forcing confession and of inwardly destroying another human being. It leads to an ego being annihilated, whereas in genuine encounter it is the ego especially that comes to the fore. The annihilation achieved by force in torture is merely a

The Adult Educator's Two Fundamental Principles

stronger form of the less noticeable negation arising in generalized and widespread situations of alienation.

Since this problem affects every level of society it should become one of the foremost professional fields in all adult learning. This is not solely a matter of being able to work and solve problems together, or of having general social capabilities which can be learnt and which have brought about much that is fruitful in social intercourse over the last fifty years. There are numerous signs now that many excellent conflict resolution methods, principles of organization development or ways of training social capabilities are becoming more and more inadequate. They remain too superficial. A deeper, more existential level in the human being must be addressed and developed in order to ensure that the many social achievements of the past fifty years can continue to be useful. What all these social capabilities are founded on is the basic ability to encounter another human being. This involves being able to experience the entirely unknown, unique individuality of the other, allowing this experience to enter one's own inner being without losing oneself in the process. Another aspect is the readiness to change oneself in consequence of this encounter between two beings.

Increasing individualization is making people harder, more one-sided and more reclusive. The remedy for all this is the endeavour to achieve genuine encounter in which an equally one-sided individual can be permitted to enter into one's own inner being, thereby breaking the spell of one's own one-sidedness. This then enables new processes of development to take place. The increasing individualization which is so heavily emphasized in today's adult education can thus be raised to a higher level that can lead to a new form of encounter amongst two or more individualities who are fundamentally different but have no need to renounce their own independence in the process. For this to happen, this new form of encounter would have to be schooled as a new faculty within adult learning. It is not hard to imagine how immeasurably important this will be for the future.

The faculty for encounter can best be researched and schooled in connection with the encounter between two individuals. However, it can also be applied much more broadly, for example in encountering nature and the earth, in encountering one's social environment or indeed all that is spiritual in the universe. Groups, organizations and whole nations can be experienced in ways that reveal their essence much more thoroughly than has been the case until now. As we have already said, this is a very important requirement for our time.

Let us consider the example of two adults who want to encounter one another properly, each one wishing to experience within his own being the otherness, the individualness of the other. From experience we know that this is a very rare occurrence (and even when it happens it is usually only partial). Mostly we only experience the other person in relation to what is already living and familiar within ourselves, and we merely believe that a real encounter has taken place. What is essentially different, what is truly foreign to ourselves, passes us by unnoticed.

Genuine encounter is an exception that can only occur in specific circumstances. In what follows a number of these preconditions will be described so that they can be purposely set up and practised. Then an attempt will be made to describe the process of encounter, and finally the goal of encounter will be discussed.

Four preconditions

1. The first precondition is that the encounter must be wanted. It involves a conscious decision made by our ego, a decision in which there is also a risk factor. Encounter involves becoming vulnerable, and there is a danger of being overwhelmed.

2. The second precondition is that one must create an *open soul space* within oneself in which the other can appear and be himself. This is actually the most difficult precondition to achieve because in many ways we are beings who only

The Adult Educator's Two Fundamental Principles

respond to external influences. There are various levels at which responses can take place, however. (See Diagram 5, p. 36.) We can distinguish between the physical level, the automatic reflex level and the soul level.

a) A physical influence, a kick for example, triggers a bruise in our physical body. The kick is followed by evasion or a counter-kick. Even merely taking one's place in a physical setting is an action that triggers a counter-action. For example two people cannot sit on the same chair at the same time.

b) Certain specific actions, such as stretching out one's hand, raising one's hat, or saying 'Good morning', trigger reflex actions which are termed conditioned reflexes.

Much of human behaviour is based on such almost automatic reflex actions. They are incorporated in the vital sphere. One example of this which provides interesting material for study is the way people have been conditioned to greet one another in their different cultures. This is the sphere of our habitual being.

c) At the soul level responses are psychological. Specific basic convictions and values, but also desires and wishes live in our soul and make us respond to external stimuli in specific ways. This has been worked out in detail by 'stimulus-response psychology'. This type of response is the most prominent one in interpersonal relationships, which is why it is frequently assumed that all human behaviour is merely a matter of responding to culturally-determined stimuli. If this were the sole truth, then genuine encounter between two human beings would not exist; in fact it would be impossible.

What we learn from the above is that as a precondition for genuine encounter we must be very familiar with the part of ourself that responds on all three levels, in order to be capable of switching it off momentarily. Only if we can do this will the open space arise in which the other person can appear in all his distinctness. This hints at a possible fourth level, one that requires some degree of psychological maturity.

Diagram 5 summarizes the three levels of response. In

36 WHAT IS ADULT LEARNING?

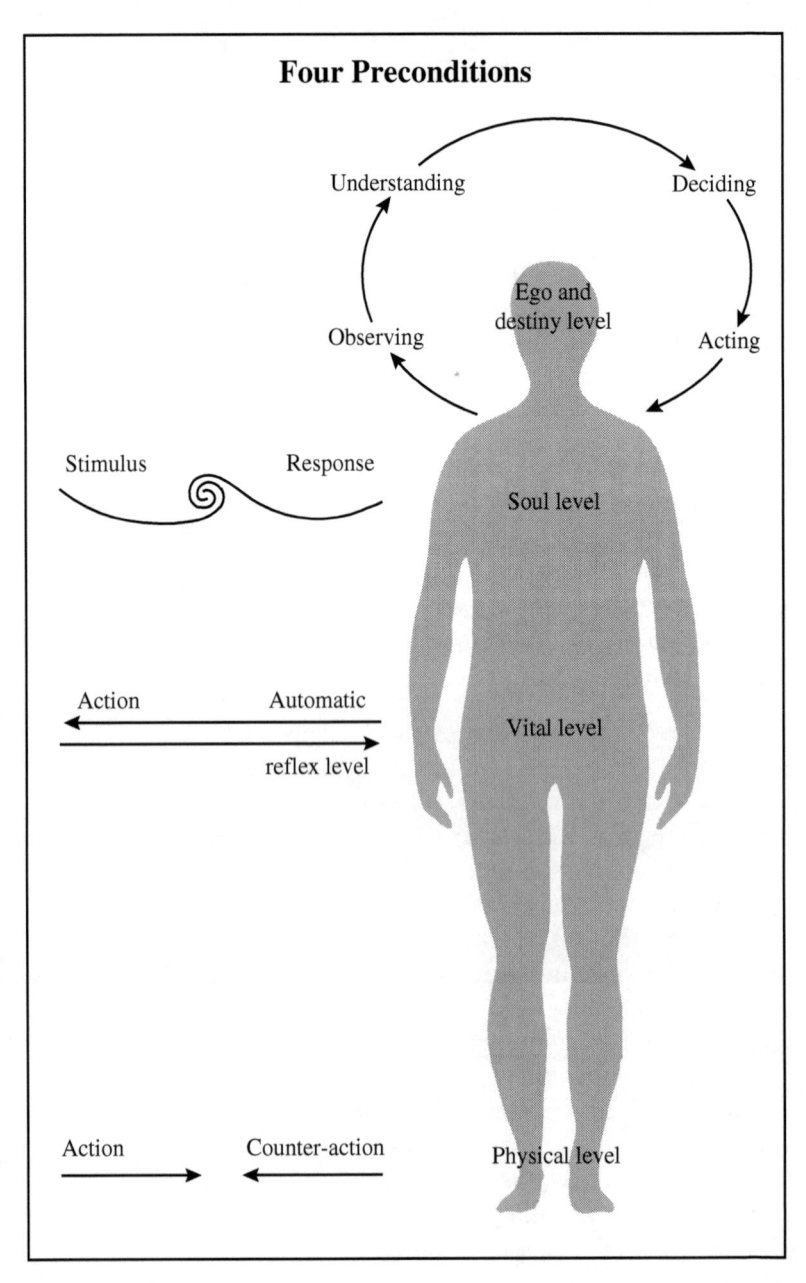

Four Preconditions

- Understanding
- Deciding
- Observing
- Acting
- Ego and destiny level
- Stimulus — Response
- Soul level
- Action — Automatic reflex level
- Vital level
- Action — Counter-action
- Physical level

Diagram 5

The Adult Educator's Two Fundamental Principles

encounter exercises between two people it helps us observe where the three levels occur, for example when you shake hands. Once you recognize them you can momentarily switch them off.

d) Momentarily switching off one's own responses calls for strong ego-forces. In this instance it is the ego that says 'No'. At the levels on which the responses normally take place this has the effect of the response being omitted. This is the place where the free, open space arises in which one can take in the other person and with the help of which one can also accept him. The capacity to do this needs practice if it is to become strong enough for us to use it whenever it appears appropriate. When the ego-encounter faculty develops, the possibility to transform the other three levels consciously begins to emerge.

3. The third precondition is that we must want the encounter, we must create an empty space where it can happen, and yet we must renounce any expectation that the other person must take part in the encounter. One cannot demand that the other person should take part in the encounter under conditions stipulated by oneself. Such an expectation would immediately create unfreedom and inhibition, and a kind of wall would rise up around the empty space. Lonely individuals often long to encounter their fellow human beings, but in exactly these circumstances such encounters cannot take place because the longing prevents them. A pseudo-encounter is then often the result. People are emotionally tuned in to one another, and get on well or work well together towards some common aim. Yet one is only experiencing oneself in and through the other person. Such experiences can be helpful and deeply satisfying at the soul level, but they are not true encounters with the unique, individual essence of the other person which can rise up in oneself as a unique, hitherto unknown experience.

There is a specific phenomenon connected with Destiny Learning that should be mentioned here.

In some encounters with people one can experience strong

feelings; memories of feelings in a way. Echoes from past incarnations accompany our sense impressions and colour the way we look at the other person. The danger is that one tends to mistake this feeling for a reality in the present moment, failing to recognize it as a memory rising up from former lives. This gives rise to a fourth precondition for encounter.

4. The fourth precondition is that one must learn to be fully present and awake within that self-created empty inner space. One needs a strengthened awareness but also a power of discernment towards everything that goes on. Our own presence of mind enables the other person to encounter us.

These four preconditions create the possibility that an encounter between two individualities can take place.

The process of encounter
Once two individuals begin to draw closer together they experience a growing insecurity. They become very vulnerable, having presented themselves without any protection and dropped all their lifelong behavioural defences. Two things can now happen. Either this feeling of insecurity develops into an experience of the abyss that generates fear, or the two of them escape into a blissful experience of togetherness that can climax as ecstasy. In the first instance everything goes rigid, they depart from the open space and the encounter is either interrupted or never takes place. In the second instance they feel wonderful, yet all they are experiencing is themselves, so that here, too, there is no true encounter.

In order to remain within the process of encounter one must continuously bring one's ego into a rhythmical alternation between establishing oneself and opening oneself to the other. The danger of losing oneself in the encounter can be overcome by a rhythmical alternation between recollecting oneself and being with the other: experience the other, experience yourself, experience the other, experience yourself. This rhythmical process can lead to a culmination in which the actual encounter takes place, which is an almost timeless occurrence that breaks through like an experience of lighting up which builds a bridge from one individual to another. An essential experience in this is: 'There is always a threshold between me as an individual and the world around me.' True encounter involves crossing this threshold momentarily.

The aim of encounter
Let us once again ask ourselves why the capacity for encounter is so important a professional field in adult learning.

Think of the encounter between two individuals described above. Even if the encounter only succeeds partially, we shall have taken into ourself something that is unique in relation to us because it has come into being through the path of another individual's development. The encounter has linked us with something new and it will become a process of healing in so far as this new, foreign element does not remain only a momentary experience but leads to a change or expansion of our own being. If this happens, the encounter will have delivered us from our one-sidedness, from our rigidity and isolation and made us more complete human beings.

Those who do not school this capacity will, in the long run, become entirely locked up in themselves or incapable of conducting their life properly. In future it will be more and more important to encounter the very essence of everything that is in the world: the earth, our fellow human beings, the universe, a plant, a stone, current events, the sun, the stars. All these call for encounter, and whenever we succeed just a little, we add a little more humanity to our own being.

When psychologists interpret human behaviour, they often use terminology or concepts belonging to the realms of the physical level or vital level when explaining psychological phenomena. This tends to cover up the real nature of the soul and also obscures the basis on which encounter takes place. This in turn leads to the creation of serious learning blockages because sight is lost not only of the soul but also of the ego as

40 WHAT IS ADULT LEARNING?

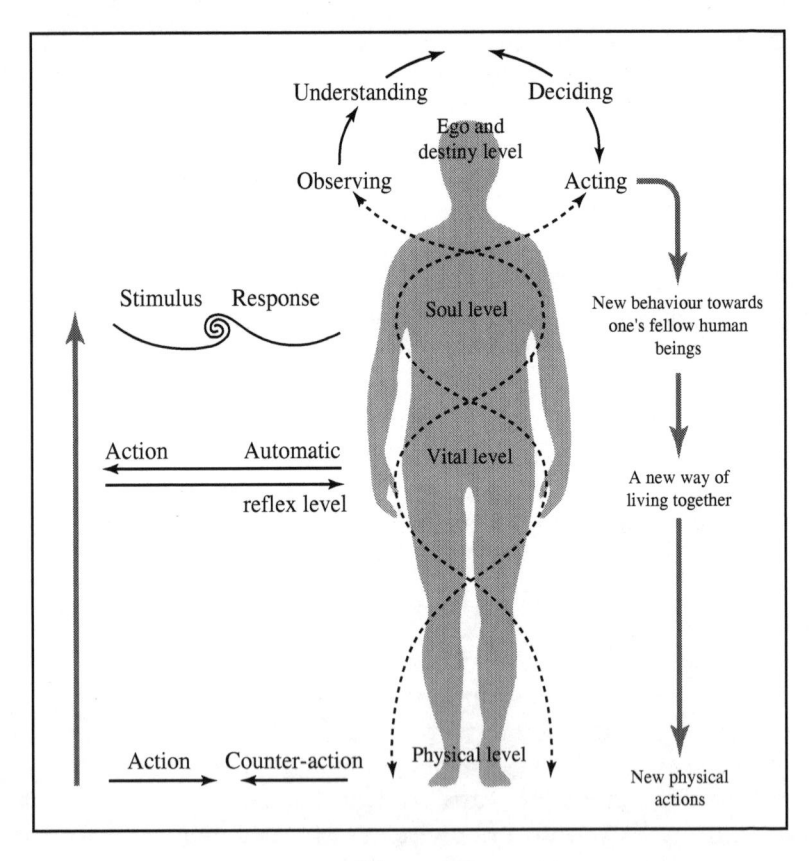

Diagram 6

the entity who is active in the encounter. All that is then left is the human being as a creature with responses only.

By contrast, when ego-activity is practised, and even if an encounter is only partially successful, this works back from the ego to the soul, vital and physical levels. Out of this can arise a new form of inter-human behaviour, for example in marriage or family life, or in the workplace. Even our physical relationships could gain an added dimension. (See Diagram 6.)

If the capacity for encounter as a conscious activity of the ego is continuously schooled and promoted during adult learning, then a relationship with the essence of the whole

The Adult Educator's Two Fundamental Principles 41

environment can arise. A number of specific ego-activities have been worked out and are described in the article by Shirley Routledge in Part Four.

It is interesting to note that in some other languages, too, the word 'encounter' expresses the overcoming of some resistance by an ego-activity. The German 'begegnen' gives the picture of working counter to something, and the French 'rencontrer' is similar. The Dutch 'ontmoeten', though, means 'one does not have to', which suggests another aspect, namely that encounter involves 'adapting to' while 'leaving the other free'.

Most of these words point to a hidden wisdom by showing that the process of encounter is one particular form of learning. This was far better understood in ancient cultures than it is today, for in those times overcoming one's opponent served not only to conquer the enemy but also to school some very exalted capacities. When you overcame your opponent you took on his distinguishing characteristics. The trials of courage among the Germanic tribes and the jousting of medieval knights served the purpose of schooling spiritual capacities. Even today's popular bullfighting is an echo of ancient initiation rites involving an extension of one's self.

In almost all initiation paths physical exercises to overcome bodily resistance led to the development of high spiritual faculties. This in itself shows the process of encounter to be one of the highest forms of learning for human beings, only nowadays encounter involves not an external fight but an inner struggle to overcome oneself, with the aim of taking into one's being something that is foreign to oneself. The faculty of encountering can become a fruitful source for many other fields of work and developing capacities.

The conscious schooling of encounter in many forms is something we urgently need, so it should be given a place in every kind of adult learning.

It is worth painting one more picture with which to close this section. The sun as our ultimate source of light casts shadows all over the earth. When sun and earth encounter one another, the shadows that arise are immensely varied and differentiated. Everything is made visible as a result of this, for we cannot actually see perfect light or absolute darkness. Similarly, if two people endeavour to encounter one another, all kinds of shadows arise because each is so different from the other. Yet it is in these ever-changing shadows that the future lives, the future that it is our task to unravel.

In the first professional field, selfless sensory observation prepared and practised the way for encounter. In forming judgements a process began which we termed 'creating an open space'. Now, in the third professional field, by schooling and practising encounter, we continue to develop that 'open space' further.

IV. Mastering, distinguishing and integrating the three learning paths

In describing the three processes of judgement forming, we experienced that the middle one, aesthetic/social or situational judgement forming, represents the heart of the three. Turning now to the three learning paths, we find that here too the middle one, Destiny Learning—self-knowledge as such—represents the heart of the three paths. Learning from destiny—the path of self-knowledge—deepens ordinary learning decisively, giving it meaning and an aim; and at the same time it also lays the foundation for Spiritual Research Learning. Destiny Learning gives both the other paths their meaning and purpose.

Treading the three learning paths
In the first section of Part One (Diagram 2) we showed that all three paths emanate from the same source, namely the seven life processes in our organism. They are nonetheless very different, as witness the three aims of understanding the world, understanding oneself, and understanding the spirit. So each of the paths must be followed and schooled separately. If they are allowed to mingle, the learning processes are adversely affected and confusion ensues. This is something the adult educator must take great care to avoid. The first learning path—including its blockages and how to

diagnose and overcome them—was described in *Awakening the Will*. Adult learners must be given the opportunity continuously to increase their learning potential, and in this way learning to learn becomes a schooling path. Individualizing adult learning generates independence, creativity and responsibility for one's own learning process.

These faculties are also the preconditions for self-knowledge, the path of Destiny Learning, for here a higher degree of independence is required. Participants in seminars in which the three learning paths were dealt with consecutively have repeatedly stressed that Destiny Learning proceeds differently, better and more thoroughly if it is preceded by learning to learn.

Spiritual Research Learning makes Destiny Learning even more objective, or, conversely, making questions of self-knowledge even more objective improves Spiritual Research Learning. This is why many adult educators stress that one must get to know the effects and meaning of karma forces very well indeed, since these play a significant part when one is researching spiritual processes.

We should still mention that blockages arising in Vocational Learning can be overcome by direct teaching methods during the learning process. In Destiny Learning the situation is different because there many blockages are a part of destiny and therefore have to be transformed. And in Spiritual Research Learning blockages and obstacles are an integral part of the research itself, for overcoming them is what yields the outcome of the research.

This shows why the three paths must be trodden separately and developed independently as far as possible, for each one follows its own inner laws. We learn to distinguish between them in order to integrate them at a higher level. This differentiation leading to integration at a higher level addresses the human being in all his wholeness.

Distinguishing between the three learning paths
When we distinguish between the three learning paths we discover that in each case an enhancement is involved. In

the first step of Vocational Learning it is observation that improves the learning potential through the proper use of the twelve senses. The first step in Destiny Learning calls for outward-looking observation right into the finest detail of sensory experience accompanied by a simultaneous exact inward-looking observation. The external and internal worlds must be sharply distinguished and brought into a relationship with one another. This is a considerable enhancement compared with the first step of Vocational Learning. Many who have not learnt how to be exact in their observation stumble at this very first step of Destiny Learning and have to be helped out by the adult educator. The first step in Spiritual Research Learning also involves observation, but here it must be observation through which we experience what comes towards us in life in such a way that we can look beyond the appearance in order to read the research question we are called upon to solve. The world around us becomes the subject matter of our research.

This example will suffice to show how important it is to distinguish between the three paths at every learning step, for much confusion can arise if we use ordinary learning processes in Destiny Learning, or if we treat spiritual research as though it were a matter of researching our personal destiny.

So first of all we have to tread the three learning paths and draw sharp distinctions between them. Having progressed sufficiently in our learning to handle all three learning paths we can then concentrate on how they are related to one another or even how they can resonate in unison.

Integrating the three learning paths
Seen in each other's context, the three learning paths obviously belong together and qualify one another. Knowledge about the world (Vocational Learning), knowledge about oneself (Destiny Learning), and knowledge of the spirit (Spiritual Research Learning) go together because it

The Adult Educator's Two Fundamental Principles

is all three in combination that address the whole human being with all his capabilities, with his connection to the world and to the spirit, and to himself. Every individual is capable of conducting spiritual research, of getting to know himself, and of making independent use of his adult learning potential in order to do justice to the demands life makes on him.

Seen from a fourth angle, the three paths appear as a unity, and it becomes evident that they complement one another very well. For example, young people who have begun practising even only the basic elements of spiritual research are able to cope with their vocational training quite differently from those who have not made this beginning.

We have already mentioned that in the way it fires the other two paths, Destiny Learning represents the heart of all three paths. Another integrating element is the fact that all three learning paths draw on the seven life processes. At the higher level it is the ego that then integrates them. It transforms the seven life processes into a threefold instrument that can grow to full stature through our learning activity.

During a seminar that presented and practised the three learning paths consecutively they and their interrelationships were evaluated by means of four questions:

1. What is the most important thing I have learnt through learning to learn (first week)?
2. What is the most important thing I have learnt through Destiny Learning (second week)?
3. What is the most important thing I have learnt through Spiritual Research Learning (third week)?
4. What has been brought into being by the three learning paths together?

We cannot here repeat all the answers received during this and similar seminars, but the answers to the fourth question were quite clear and are shown here:

1. The three paths belong together.
2. They deepen, support and complement one another.
3. Therefore one should not set out on one learning path without treading the other two as well.
4. This threefold learning for adults has sown the seeds of a new and necessary way of adult learning. Some participants called it the foundation stone of a type of learning that befits our present age.

Another essential point is that the three learning paths have a healing effect when they are combined in adult learning. Vocational Learning without self-knowledge or spiritual research can lead to 'blinkered professionalism'. Destiny Learning that is pursued without 'learning to learn as an adult' or the objectivy of Research Learning can lead to delusions about oneself. On the other hand, Destiny Learning can have a healing effect on the other two learning paths because self-knowledge can signal and overcome one-sidedness, fixations, illusions, obsessions, or any other aberrations that can accompany the other two.

Combining the three learning paths is, moreover, essential for one's further path in life. A good vocational training or university course completed between the ages of 20 and 30 can initially provide support in one's professional life, but it can easily cause an individual to get stuck in a professional deformation in the second half of life. The second learning path is particularly helpful here, since it uncovers and transforms one's one-sidedness, rigidity and illusions. Over and above this, the basic attitude of research helps one adapt one's professional practice to new circumstances and renew it creatively in other ways.

For the adult educator this means that inwardly he must be able to integrate the three paths and base his professional work on that union. Outwardly he can then use them in different ways, which means that he will endeavour to create many and varied learning situations. This is something that makes considerable demands on *how* adult learning is conducted.

The relationship between the ability to encounter (III) and the synthesis of the three learning paths (IV)

The third professional field involves learning the ability to encounter, while in the fourth the ability to create a synthesis between the three learning paths is schooled. It is difficult to comprehend and thus also to express what might arise out of a relationship between the encounter ability and a synthesis of the three learning paths. At first sight the two appear to be very different qualitatively. Encounter needs openness and an inner space; it involves taking something foreign into ourselves, this being a rather feminine quality. In contrast, the three learning paths are more knowledge-oriented and have their activity directed outwards, which is a rather masculine quality. Together, the two can bring about the birth of something new. Encounter creates spiritually an 'open space', and this open space can be entered and filled from the outside by the independent human spirit that develops when the three learning paths are followed.

Encounter and synthesis of the three learning paths also, however, have one thing in common: the formation of destiny. Every encounter, whether it is a success or not, creates destiny. The path of Destiny Learning brings about the recognition of destiny, whereupon it can be worked on and transformed. Combining these two elements, recognition of destiny and shaping destiny, then makes it possible to bring healing and creative order into destiny as a whole. One can also say that the newly-arising space in the centre becomes filled by the independent human spirit in Vocational Learning. It achieves reflection and self-knowledge through Destiny Learning. And it is carried by the basic attitude of Spiritual Research Learning.

In this sense adult learning will have to enable a new individual central strength to be born in every human soul.

Looking beyond our immediate horizon for a moment, this statement can give us an inkling of how this 'new quality', if it could be made integral to all forms of education and learning, might gradually lead to a new identity for Europe—Europe as the middle between East and West. A force would arise that would be strong enough to create a healing balance between Asia and the western world. This need not mean that the East as such and the West as such should not also each seek out their own specific middle. After all, China calls herself the Middle Kingdom!

V. Day-time learning
Our day-time learning takes place either in a teaching situation or during daily practice. These two have unfortunately grown further and further apart, so that the relevance of what is taught in colleges and the like to what is needed in professional and general practice has become exceedingly questionable.

One cause (among many) of this split is a lack of understanding about how one can learn through one's work, through life experience and through doing one's own research. Another cause lies in the one-sided over-emphasis on theoretical information on the one hand and the training of skills based on pre-designed models on the other.

The three learning paths provide an answer to these contemporary problems. Following them can increasingly narrow the gap between theory and practice because they enable the adult learner to become a mature, responsible and creative individual with regard to his own work, his own being and the spiritual background to life. This is entirely different from merely absorbing knowledge and perhaps only partially digesting it. The three learning paths transform us into self-learning and self-developing individuals.

Day-time and night-time learning have an important contribution to make when we want to integrate the three learning paths. This is even the case in Vocational Learning, for although it is focussed on day-time learning and has its aims on our side of the threshold it is often deepened and improved imperceptibly by night-time learning.

With Destiny Learning this is more obvious because here the spiritual and physical, the sense-perceptible and supersensible constantly interweave. Night-time learning can then

The Adult Educator's Two Fundamental Principles

become something through which the two worlds are consciously brought together.

In Spiritual Research Learning we ask the questions during our daily life, but the answers come from beyond the threshold. Here night-time learning attains its greatest importance in combination with day-time learning.

What applies to the three learning paths separately is even more relevant when they are integrated. Their integration takes place to the same degree as we manage to combine day-time and night-time learning.

How do day-time and night-time learning interweave in Vocational Learning? All learning is based on struggling with resistances. We live in a physical body in a physical world; these provide the resistance through which our consciousness can develop. By trying to deal with our physical reality we encounter a huge variety of resistances. Our mental, emotional and bodily activities wrestle with these outer and inner resistances. In contrast with this, when we simply accept and repeat learning material offered by others, and when we copy methods according to instructions, this is more like a kind of conditioning that misses the point of genuine adult learning.

This still does not explain why our conscious struggle against resistances can be transformed into the formation of spiritual faculties that come to expression as gifts, talents, abilities, genius even. The process of transformation takes place during the night, beyond our day-time consciousness. We sleep, yet the learning process continues, but now without the resistances of the day-time. Countless observations have shown that something happens to us during the night. Not only do we afterwards awake refreshed, but something has changed psychologically and spiritually as well. This points to a link between day-time and night-time learning about which more will be said in the coming two sections.

Adult educators wishing to develop the professional field of day-time learning might like to ask themselves what forms of learning can be applied in order to assist adult learners, so that they:

1. more and more become observers of their own learning processes,
2. more and more come to experience inwardly their own learning processes,
3. more and more become researchers of their own learning processes.

If this is what is needed, then it is obvious that most of the subjects taught for the purpose of sitting examinations are unsuitable since they are confined to what can be compared, measured or computerized. The above questions, however, point to how the adult learner can be helped to notice his own progress and realize how it has been achieved, thus enabling him constantly to improve his own progress independently. Independence will grow to the same extent that observing and assessing one's own learning grows. Then day-time learning becomes a conscious schooling path.

Methods such as evaluations, previews and reviewing one's day backwards may be used. All these can be further developed and refined. Another aid to observation is the individual learning diary. A large step forward becomes possible when one has found a way of evaluating day-time learning in a manner that transforms it into sustenance for night-time learning, since this gives an extra boost to the next day's learning process.

(More on this in the next section.)

VI. Night-time learning

To claim that we learn while we sleep may initially sound absurd. Yet many observations have shown that it is also not true to maintain that nothing at all happens during the night to influence our day-time learning. Many of us have noticed on awakening that yesterday's problems appear to have solved themselves, that some disagreement is cleared up, or that we suddenly know what to do next. People often find their best ideas coming to them as they wake up, and even keep a notebook and pencil by the bed so that they can immediately note down what they have brought back with them from the night. These people are already practising night-time learning.

For example, basic moods such as expectations regarding the coming day, depression, satisfaction, pangs of conscience, restlessness and so on that assail us when we wake up can frequently not be explained by reference to what happened the day before. This is another sign that we continue to learn during the night, digesting and evaluating what went on yesterday. Psychologists know that blows of destiny often take several days and nights to digest.

So it makes good sense to say: 'I must sleep on this before making up my mind.' Of course conscious day-time learning ceases during the night, but our unconscious continues to work, undisturbed by sense impressions and intellectual interpretations. In fact, the night is often much more sensible than the day! So if we want to take the full learning process into account, we have to include night-time learning as well.

Experiments have shown that our learning capacity can be greatly enhanced by making use of the day-time/night-time learning cycle. Begin by concentrating on waking up. You will soon notice that the answers to questions such as 'How did I wake up? What did I experience? What came into my mind?' become increasingly relevant the more you practise. You will also increasingly have intuitive ideas during the day-time, which shows how your searches and efforts of the day before have been continuing in your unconscious.

We have already said that night-time learning is important for all three learning paths. In Spiritual Research Learning, however, it occupies pride of place because during the day we live in the sense world where we enjoy an awareness of outer objects, whereas at night we are in a spiritual world where our consciousness is spiritual and therefore qualitatively different. Our senses and our normal intellect no longer work there, and we are surrounded by spiritual beings. It is from this world that the answers come to the questions we ask during our spiritual research. Transitions from day to night and night to day involve crossing a threshold of consciousness of which we can become increasingly aware as time goes on. This brings about the full unfolding of adult learning.

By 'threshold of consciousness' we mean the following. On the one hand there is a psychological threshold between our conscious and our unconscious life of soul, and on the other there is also an external threshold we encounter with our senses. There is a supersensible, spiritual world both in our unconscious and behind sense-perceptible phenomena. So spiritual experiences can involve crossing the threshold either inwardly or outwardly. Night-time learning is a form of learning that can teach us the meaning and value of everything we do during the day. Both our sense of truth and our conscience in its true form live in us especially intensively during night-time learning. Thus moral learning and the forming of moral judgements take place mainly during night-time learning. In the day-time this can then resonate in the form of new insights or as the voice of conscience. Both stem from the same source but we experience them in different ways. Our sense of truth evaluates our thoughts over against the universal, uniform world of thought; the voice of our conscience is our personal evaluation of our actions over against the divine harmony of the universe.

The adult educator is now faced with a difficult decision as to whether he wants to and indeed is able to take into his teaching the two thresholds to be crossed in going to sleep and waking up. He may well ask whether it is really necessary to do so.

Contemporary phenomena can help us find the answer. We can observe that spiritual experiences are increasingly impinging on our day-time consciousness, often unexpectedly and inexplicably. People hear voices, experience (invisible) pictures, unusual dreams, vague and obscure emotions. In other words, our consciousness is already intertwined with many supersensible experiences. The threshold between day and night is growing more transparent. One third of adult seminar participants regularly have supersensible experiences; a second third are familiar with such experiences to some extent, while the remainder find it difficult to ascertain whether they have such experiences or not because they are so intangible.

The fact is that humanity at present crosses this threshold semi-consciously and is undergoing a transformation of consciousness. Adult education must take this fact into account. Therefore we cannot avoid taking on night-time learning as an important professional field.

There is one more crucial question, and that is: How does night-time learning come about? We know the answer for day-time learning, but with regard to night-time learning we shall have to consult the latest scientific findings as well as spiritual science because our night-time learning is cared for by spiritual beings while we spend the night in the spiritual world. With our day-time learning we create the preconditions and prepare the working material for the night. Let me recommend the book *Der Schlaf und seine Bedeutung* ('Sleep and its Meaning') by Stefan Leber as a very helpful resource on this subject.[5]

The bridge between day-time learning (V) and night-time learning (VI)

The bridge between day-time and night-time learning is built by the way we evaluate our day in the evening and by the way we harvest the yield of night-time learning next morning.

In evaluating the day it is helpful to imagine a sunset mood that generates a feeling of peacefulness in us. The sun has shone upon everything we did, said and thought during the day. So in the picture we imagine, the sun appears as a kind of cosmic conscience evaluating our day-time activities and the contribution we have made—even when the weather is bad. At the same time the sun can also awaken gratitude in us for all that has been given us during the day, for what we have experienced and learnt, and how we coped. This basic mood of conscience and gratitude creates the soil on which night-time learning can grow. Many questions arise in us, and the adult educator must find all kinds of expressions and methods by which to stimulate this rather more moral evaluation that is to accompany the concrete question: 'What have I learnt?'

At the beginning of the next day we then harvest, or bring into our consciousness, the yield of our night-time learning. We do this by trying to make a connection with the previous day in order to experience what the night has added to it. As already mentioned, this usually takes the form of unexpected ideas, dreams, evaluating moods, images, words or sentences which can also continue to make their appearance later on during the whole day. It is helpful to pay regular close attention to the moment of waking up and to observe how the transition from night to day takes place.

The most important thing in all this is to make these sudden ideas, dreams and so on into a part of adult learning, whereby the most difficult task is to retain the yield of night-time learning in one's consciousness. Step V in Vocational Learning—exercising (the metamorphosis of maintaining)—must be carried out regularly. The organic process of maintaining is a kind of night-time regeneration that replaces the break-down and tiredness of the day. In Vocational Learning it becomes a supportive process of spiritual regeneration that strengthens our day-time learning. This happens because night-time learning is qualitatively quite different from day-time learning. Day-time learning is primarily determined by sense impressions, whereas during the night the process is a moral one. That is why the manner in which the evening evaluation of the day is carried out creates the bridge by which the morning contemplation can bring what has been learnt during the night into the beginning of the new day. The evening evaluation builds the bridge leading from day to night; and harvesting the yield of the night builds the bridge leading from night to day. They qualify and strengthen one another.

All this creates a 24-hour rhythm of night and day. The 24-hour rhythm is the rhythm of our ego, which is the most important one for adult learning. Our ego-awareness is heightened by this ego-rhythm. It teaches us to sleep differently and to be awake differently. Day-time learning will increasingly qualify night-time learning, and night-time learning will increasingly fructify day-time learning. Slowly but surely a kind of continuous consciousness will arise. Then

The Adult Educator's Two Fundamental Principles

we learn to live on both sides of reality, on the sense-perceptible, physical side and on the spiritual, moral side. In a perfectly natural manner we then discover the modern schooling path which, as we have seen, is actually a modern method of spiritual research.

By schooling day-time learning in combination with night-time learning we create the conditions we need in order to cope with the threshold situation mentioned earlier; or, put another way, the threshold situation itself becomes a process of adult learning for every individual human being.

As we have seen, the value of what we learn each day is determined by the moral quality of what we have thought and spoken and the way we have acted on that day. To think, to speak and to act meaningfully—these are gifts with which every child is born; they are what makes us truly human when we use them as adults.

Each day we can ask ourselves seriously what use we have made of our memories and inner pictures and of the thoughts on which these are based. As adult learners we are right to question whether we have improved and shaped in a meaningful and living way this gift of thought which helps us communicate with one another about the world around us. Was there an ideal element in our mental pictures or were they, on the contrary, merely self-serving and routine, abstract and untrue considerations that have devalued us in the eyes of the spiritual world?

We can ask ourselves similar questions about the way we have spoken, for the gift of language is degenerating nowadays. It is astonishing to find how much of what is spoken no longer has any living content, or does not serve communication with other human beings. How much remains unheard or is indeed inaudible because it lacks content and has nothing to do with communication? One can ask oneself: 'How have I used my gift of language today? Were my words meaningful, helpful, healing; did they bring people together, solve problems or release tension? Did I fill my words with real ideas owing to the fact that language unites my inner world with my environment?' One can also ask oneself what one has heard and taken in by way of essential information. Questioning the way we have used language leads us to insights about how we have treated our fellow human beings on this day; it also helps us evaluate the feelings we have had.

Querying our actions is different, for we change the world whenever we do something; our actions are written into the universe. Whether we fell trees or build a house, buy something or pay our debts, whether we do as we intended, whether we act in a creative, social way—from the smallest to the greatest deed, each one has consequences outside of ourselves. When we evaluate our actions at the end of the day we become aware of our impulse for improvement, for whatever we have done we could have done better. It also deepens our capacity for forming moral judgements (whereas when we evaluate language the capacity for aesthetic judgement is called for, as is the capacity for cognitive judgement when we evaluate thoughts).

When we thus evaluate our day-time learning with regard to these three gifts and consider how we have handled them during the day, we are creating fertile soil for night-time learning. This is because we take with us into the night all the many open or unanswered questions of our thinking as well as the manner in which we have dealt with our language and with our social environment. We harvest the yield of our day-time learning by finding in it much that is fruitful and much that remains unanswered. Night-time learning can then provide the answers, let things grow or correct them.

One good way of beginning the evaluation is to harvest the yield of night-time learning each morning. Ask yourself questions like: 'How am I feeling now that I have woken up? What have I brought with me from the night? How do today's thoughts, feelings and wishes for action differ from those I had yesterday?' If, for example, the participants in a seminar tell each other their night-time learning experiences each day, there will quite soon be an increase in their awareness of night-time learning, and the whole learning process will be speeded up. It is important, though, to support this night-time learning in the morning by giving introductions about the two

The Adult Educator's Two Fundamental Principles 57

transitions across the threshold: going to sleep and waking up. The process differs from one individual to another, so there are many variations. It is also important to speak about what actually happens during the life of the night.

We can add that the backwards review, the evaluation and the preview are also very helpful for assessing longer processes such as a week-long seminar, a whole semester, or even longer projects. For direct day-time and night-time learning, on the other hand, the moral evaluation of our thought life, our use of words and our actions is more to the point. The reason for this is that night-time learning evaluates these three faculties especially because the spiritual beings who gave us these gifts of walking, using language and thus also thinking during the first three years of our childhood now evaluate every night what the adult has made of his day-time learning process, in order to strengthen, carry further and inspire everything of value for the next day. The split between our day-time and our night-time consciousness ensures that we can always retain our independence as learners, while the spiritual beings determine and prepare during our night-time learning how and what we are to learn in order to become more human in the future.

It happens quite often that unconscious or semi-conscious anxieties arise at the threshold between day and night because as we glide into the unconsciousness of night we lose our day-time consciousness and the inner security it gives us. Insomnia is often the consequence of being unable to let go of the day, so that we remain in a state of suspended animation. Frequently used but inappropriate remedies for this are:

1. inducing a state of total exhaustion in order to 'go out like a light';
2. watching television: we keep our senses on the move without making any effort and so remain artificially awake, taking in images that have nothing to do with the real events of the day and can thus not be worked through during the night;
3. taking alcohol, sleeping pills and so on.

The adult educator should realize that he can help many people in this matter by encouraging them to evaluate their day-time learning, thus creating a suitable basic mood for the night. By evaluating the learning processes we lose our fear of the night because if we honestly assess our day we need no longer be anxious about the judgement likely to be passed on us by the spiritual world.

At the threshold leading from night to day we are often assailed by mild depression, feelings of hopelessness or powerlessness that make it difficult for us to begin the new day. If we face up to this energetically in order to discover what hints it may hold for the coming day, or whether it has something to do with what happened the day before, we can easily overcome this feeling of uncertainty. Here too the adult educator can give a great deal of help in building up a sound and healthy way of dealing with life's problems.[6]

VII. Ability to manage the sevenfold learning process independently

This chapter began with a description of how the adult educator must develop the two fundamental principles or capabilities (awakening the will to learn and generating the sense of truth) and the seven professional fields as the basis for an adult learning that is appropriate for our time. We now come to the seventh professional field, which is actually the adult learner's main instrument that will enable him to cultivate and shape the learning process independently. This instrument is created when the seven life processes in our organism, where they function in accordance with natural laws, are transformed by our personal activity into conscious learning processes. These processes must be mastered by constant practice until they are permanently at our disposal whenever we need them.

The seven life processes serve the life in our body. The seven learning processes serve the life of our spirit. Our ego transforms the life processes into learning processes. In so far as we succeed in this, we can learn as adults. In so far as we fail, any learning we do remains bound up with our body and leads to automatism, dressage or conditioning, with traits belonging to the animal world.

In every teaching method we should ask in connection with each one of the seven processes whether the life processes have been made properly human by our ego so as to be available as instruments for our psychological and spiritual development. If this is indeed the case, then adult learning—which was at first merely a more or less instinctive matter—becomes a fully conscious, self-responsible learning process.

In their very shape, in the way they follow one after the other, the seven learning processes combine to form another process which proceeds initially from the outside inwards before turning outwards again after it has become individualized. In Steps I and II (observing and relating), cognitive judgement forming is more to the fore, while Steps III, IV and V (digesting, individualizing and exercising) make more use of aesthetic, situational judgement forming, and Steps V, VI and VII (exercising, growing and creative appplication) incline more towards the moral element in judgement forming.

It is important for the adult educator to realize that the seven life processes are a law of nature. They maintain our life, they are our life, and if one of them does not work properly we fall ill. The same goes for learning. If one of the processes does not work properly we have a learning deficiency (so the expression 'learning diagnosis' is quite appropriate in this connection). One of the aims of the adult educator is to enable self-responsible development to come about. If he learns to transform the seven life processes into learning processes and thus overcome the learning deficiencies and blockages, then this will provide a basis on which his teaching can become healthy and supportive for any human being's development. The adult educator then becomes an instrument serving the development of the adult learner.

If the participants initially practise taking regular account of the seven learning processes, this may at first appear to be a regimented, pre-planned manner of proceeding. Experience has shown, however, that if one does not lose sight of the links between the learning processes and the living source (the life processes), then this learning gradually comes to be experienced as a process of nourishing one's spiritual development. One then comes to know exactly whether one has really digested something or whether one has only taken it in and believed it without actually having individualized it. One can sense whether one has merely taken something in without digesting and individualizing it since this leads to merely automatic actions when putting it into practice.

The self-responsibility and self-guidance acquired in Vocational Learning increases considerably in Destiny Learning and is enhanced even further in Spiritual Research Learning. The foundation for the seven learning processes should be laid right at the beginning of Vocational Learning, otherwise the other two learning paths cannot be built up in a healthy way.

Conclusion

It is appropriate to mention here the application of the seven learning processes in psychotherapy, consultancy work and artistic therapy (see also Part Four).

A sevenfold learning path that existed in antiquity was seen to be linked to the seven planets, each of which possessed its own treasure-house of wisdom. In the late Middle Ages this path flourished in a new form at the School of Chartres, where it was taught in the form of the seven liberal arts inspired by the seven divine virgins revealed to the teachers at Chartres. These seven liberal arts enabled one to build a spiritual chariot in which one could journey to heaven. Those who had succeeded in building this chariot were then permitted to instruct others. Although the Chartres School ceased to exist it nevertheless remained for many the archetypal manifestation of true adult learning.

Today, however, human beings learn quite differently. External observation and also the scientific explanation of facts belong to the modern age. Human beings have become head-people. Learning no longer arises out of revelations from above mediated by divine virgins; it comes about when life processes are awakened in the human being. We create our own sevenfold path by transforming these life processes, and this takes place in three ways: along the path of worldly knowledge (Vocational Learning), along the path of self-knowledge (Destiny Learning), and along the path of spiritual knowledge (Spiritual Research Learning). It is as though the great School of Chartres were to arise again, but now built up from within in seven learning processes that tread a threefold path.

The seven professional fields today also provide a suitable structure for general preparatory courses or college foundation years. They could provide participants with a basic adult education that would develop the capabilities of the seven professional fields as a foundation for adult learning throughout life.

People are increasingly in need of a basic education of this kind in order to cope with both the inner psychological challenges and the external life situations that confront them in our time. The points of emphasis in a schooling such as this must of course differ depending on where it is being applied, whether in Europe, in the East or West, in the North or South. Didactic guidance will also vary in different parts of the world. But the basic schooling itself, being a matter of general relevance to humanity as a whole, remains the same the world over.

For this to come about, adult educators will need to become far more professional in this respect than they are today. They could, for example, examine their own development on a regular basis with regard to the seven professional fields. 'Which of the professional fields have I worked on the most, and which the least? Where do I still have considerable gaps? Which of my professional fields have I developed thoroughly but one-sidedly? Which have I developed from many angles but superficially?' A learning and research plan can be put together on the basis of the answers to these questions. In making this evaluation it is fruitful to confront the seven professional fields with each other, to move them in and out of each other and let them converse together, for all seven are interlinked. Interrelating the fields in different ways has often led to the unexpected discovery of new methods, connections and insights.

Another schooling question to be asked is: 'To what extent are these seven professional fields still only a working concept or model rather than a living organism from which I can always draw new ideas?' Here is an example:

1. An encounter between the use of the senses (Field I) and the three judgement processes (Field II) creates an open space in us between our inner and our outer world. Not until this open space arises can we observe and form independent judgements selflessly.
2. The capacity to encounter others (Field III) and the judgement processes (Field II) have to be combined, and only when this has happened can this middle space come to birth and then begin to develop properly. The capacity to encounter others (Field III) nourishes this middle space, and the threefold learning paths (Field IV) also develop this middle space. In all this, it is always the human being who works to maintain the balance between the inner and the outer world.
3. When the human being is in balance like this, and with the help of the rhythmical processes of day-time and night-time learning (Fields V and VI), life on both sides of reality can begin to arise. Earthly and spiritual reality can now connect in a fruitful way and thus guarantee the future of our civilization. Field VII, which involves the transformation of the life processes into the learning processes, is the source and fertile soil for all the other Professional Fields.

Part Two:
Destiny Learning

1. General Introduction to Destiny Learning

Destiny comprises on the one hand the pleasant and unpleasant events that affect us in life, and on the other the instinctive manner in which we respond to them in our own, almost compulsively individual way. There appears to be an inevitability about destiny, as though it emanated from some unknown power. It is a reality in our lives, a reality we experience as inscrutable. However, this way of experiencing destiny changes the moment we begin to regard it as a learning situation we are being offered, a chance to learn how we can change ourselves and thus take a hand in shaping our future. When we treat destiny as a learning situation it becomes a reality in which we can live consciously.

We have a destiny, we live in our destiny, and we weave our destiny ourselves. Destiny is the reality in which we live, but since we do not live consciously within this reality it remains hidden from view. This is borne out when we consider our biography, for it appears to us as a picture. (This even forms the basis on which some therapies are founded.) It is insufficient explanation, however, as to why our destiny is as it is, let alone what the meaning of the laws of destiny might be. We can think up as many and varied explanations as we like regarding why some relationships succeed while others fail, why we find ourselves in some conflict situation or other, what our good or bad luck means, or indeed why we are as we are. But without a proper answer such explanations remain nothing more than a web of illusions, a *fata Morgana*, a mirage of constructed interpretations. They fail to touch on the 'whys and wherefores' of destiny. Adults have to address these questions if they want to learn from their destiny. Learning from destiny entails recognizing the 'whys and wherefores' so as to live increasingly in reality and manage life ever more fruitfully and meaningfully.

It is the concept of reincarnation that helps us get to the root of why destiny (karma) is as it is, and in addition we also need some knowledge of the processes that take place in the life we lead between death and a new birth. If we do not wish to step beyond the boundaries of our earthly life we shall be unable to unravel the secrets of its reality, continuing instead to blunder about blindly in a world of semblance. The way towards genuine self-knowledge and thus also spiritual knowledge will remain closed to us.

Is a new way of 'learning from destiny' really needed today? Is the time ripe for such a new way? There are many phenomena that seem to be answering this question in the affirmative. The subjects of reincarnation and karma are appearing more and more frequently in literature as well as in works on spiritual science. There is a proliferation of books and lectures by individuals who give vivid descriptions of past lives or who have had a near death experience and discuss ways of 'coming back'. Such experiences are also being increasingly included in psychotherapy. Many people have had experiences connected with reincarnation, and awareness of karma is on the increase, as is the belief that reincarnation is the only way of explaining the tremendous variety that exists amongst human beings and their destinies.

If we regard the experiences people are having in this respect as a reality, then our concept of human development requires to be extended by this important further dimension of reincarnation and karma. To regard a person's life as a sequence of coincidences is then no longer tenable. If such experiences continue to be pushed to one side instead of being worked through in our everyday life and learning, we shall soon be facing a disastrous increase in psychological disorders. (Many psychotherapists are already diagnosing such disorders as undigested old karma.) In ordinary life, too, it is becoming more and more necessary for our general mental health that every adult should come to grips with 'learning from destiny'. The time is ripe for this; in fact it is high time, given the general increase in psychological confusion resulting from inexplicable experiences.

General Introduction to Destiny Learning 67

If reincarnation and karma are realities, this means not only that our actions in long-past incarnations helped to change the world but also that we ourselves have learned through working in that way at changing the world. It means that at any moment in our present life these actions can return to us, so that in our present destiny we shall come up against the consequences of what we ourselves did in earlier lives. In our destiny we encounter ourselves, for our destiny lives in the human beings and circumstances that now surround us. Many of the people we now meet have lived with us before; they too have learnt and changed, having worked on their former actions in the life between death and rebirth.

People who meet each other in their present life come up against the consequences of former actions, but now they are equipped with new capabilities, new possibilities and changed karmic opportunities. While a destiny event or a meeting with someone can thus often be regarded as the consequence of something in a past life, we must also realize that every destiny event, every successful or unsuccessful relationship, is also the cause of future consequences. One could call this the 'logic of karma' in contrast to the 'logic of a psychology' that regards causes and effects as being restricted to a single lifetime only.

The core aspect of any learning process involves transforming one's destiny out of an awareness of reincarnation and karma, for it is through this that one plants new seeds for the future. Every one of us can change from merely bearing our destiny to transforming it, and again from transforming our destiny to creating it. We can become participators in the evolution of human beings and humanity. Every healthy adult is capable of coming to grips with this learning process. The more we learn through it, the more we can change from being creatures to being co-creators. Reincarnation is the gift of development; the laws of karma are the strategy of development.

There is something astonishing waiting to be discovered in all this: the shaping of destiny, our karma, turns out to be a wonderful 'adult education programme', a far wiser one than we could ever have devised ourselves. One of the laws of karma is that of self-knowledge; karmic situations are brought into play to give us the possibility of self-knowledge. Destiny is a gift from the gods that enables us to move on from being no more than a creature to becoming a fully responsible co-creator of world evolution—if we want to learn from destiny.

In order to do this we must learn to recognize the forces of destiny, to transform them within ourselves, for we are our own self-created destiny and should learn to answer creatively the questions posed by the world. Every event of destiny contains a question to which we can find the reply. If we can recognize every event as a consequence of the past and a cause of the future, then an open space is created in which the decision is taken as to how we should deal with this present situation. We must pay equal attention to both sequences of events: past causes of the present situation must be recognized, and future consequences of our actions must be taken into account. The seven steps of Destiny Learning we are about to discuss aim to help us act creatively when encountering destiny events.

The general adult learning process derived from the seven life processes has been modified for Destiny Learning, as will be described in detail in the following. By way of a survey the seven life processes are shown here once more, accompanied by the seven steps of Destiny Learning:

General Introduction to Destiny Learning

Life Processes	Learning Processes	Destiny Learning Processes
I Breathing	Observing	Step I—Observing a destiny event
II Warming	Relating	Step II—Connecting it with one's biography
III Nourishing	Digesting	Step III—Finding the causes and discovering one's learning task
IV Secreting (sorting)	Individualizing	Step IV—Accepting one's destiny
V Maintaining	Exercising	Step V—Practising in daily life
VI Growing	Growing capabilities	Step VI—Growing sense of destiny
VII Reproducing	Creating	Step VII—Creating order in one's destiny

2. Destiny is the Reality in Which We Live

Let us add some general thoughts before looking in detail at the individual steps of Destiny Learning.

Destiny is the reality in which we live. We can begin to live consciously in this reality and also discover our tasks for the future when we understand our destiny, its origins in former lives and how we digest it in the life between death and a new birth.

Much is nowadays spoken and written about karma and reincarnation, and many people study what Rudolf Steiner and others have had to say on the subject. Yet it is still rare for anyone to reach conclusions as to how one might take karma into account while living one's own everyday life.

If we do not understand our own tasks or recognize why events and encounters in our destiny take place in one way and not in another, we fail to live in reality, deluding ourselves with regard to our own life and misjudging our fellow human beings. How can we form an accurate opinion about people and their actions if we know nothing about the karmic forces working within and towards them? How can we achieve genuine self-knowledge without recognizing our own karmic origins?

Self-knowledge is karma-knowledge. Psychological interpretations that take only our present life into account, our biography between birth and death, are insufficient, although biography work can open doors for karmic self-knowledge.

A path of learning for karmic self-knowledge, Destiny Learning, has now been discovered and will be enlarged on here. It has already been described and tried out for some considerable time in various places in Germany, as well as in Britain, Holland, Finland, South Africa and elsewhere.

This path is founded on the adult human being's ability to learn independently and objectively. Those who are unable in their present situation to tread such a path independently will need the expert guidance of a counsellor well-versed in

Destiny is the Reality in Which We Live 71

the practice of destiny. This applies, for example, to individuals whose perceptive faculties are inadequate, or who find it difficult to distinguish between inner and outer experiences, or who tend to form judgements that are heavily subjective or projective, in short those who cannot embark on adult learning in a self-responsible way. For such situations, a number of successful variations of this schooling, involving counselling, have grown up over the years.

The learning path of self-knowledge is based on the independent learning process of the adult human being. We could call it 'the second adult learning path'.

Would it not be sensible in future to include this 'second learning path' in every adult learning situation? This would certainly pose a challenge for the adult educator, but it can be done and taught! When all is said and done, what is the point of a good specialist training if the trainees are still stuck in illusions about themselves and remain unable to observe the reality in which they live?

Destiny Learning begins with a destiny event that has actually happened and can therefore be observed; this is our only firm point of reference. No interpretation, presentiment, dream, nebulous sensation—even any supersensible experience not founded on concrete observation—can be used as the starting point of an adult learning process of this kind. In this sense the starting point of Step I is no different from that of any normal learning. The subject, our destiny, is what is exceptional. We ourselves are the subject that is to be learnt, for the aim of this learning is self-knowledge as a continuous developmental activity. Life provides us with material in the form of events; and more material is supplied by our way of dealing with those events. By objectively observing both of these we can arrive at an initial form of self-knowledge.

In what follows the seven steps of Destiny Learning will be described in more detail, for these are the steps that can help us come to grips with this learning. The description will serve as a general prototype of the Destiny Learning process, bearing in mind that variations of this prototype can be envisaged. At the same time it will also demonstrate how this process can be tackled within the framework of a seminar when four to five individuals meet who want to set out along this path together and support one another in doing so.

(Although work in small groups has proved successful and achievable, it should not be regarded as the only method. For organizations, or 'encounter conversations', and also in connection with various therapies, there are several methods by which one can proceed and accompany the participants through the seven Learning Steps.)

The blockages and hindrances likely to be encountered at each stage will also be described, as will measures that can be undertaken to support the process.

Learning Step I

1. Observing a destiny event

The event may be a meeting with someone, a happening in our family or at work, an unexpected discovery, an accident, a surprise or anything else. It occurs at the crossing point of two or more chains of events, but we may not be fully aware of what all these mean. All we know about is what we have observed with our senses and what inner feelings and emotions it called forth. We are not able to observe in the same way how the event affected any of the other people involved in it, nor what their feelings were. This shows that every destiny event, especially when others are involved as well, represents a crossing point in a web of destiny of which we are vaguely aware but cannot yet see clearly. We shall only gradually begin to see this web more clearly when we reach Step V of the learning path we are on, when we begin to practise consciously within actual life situations.

Even in Step I, though, we are already doing something with our destiny. We are observing it as minutely as we can, we are starting to be active with regard to our destiny, we are willing to observe it both in its outward happenings and its inward processes. As we watch both these aspects, the inner and the outer, a third element begins to speak to us. This speaking is the language of destiny, and it gives us a feeling of astonishment. At that moment we feel: 'Something is happening that is profoundly connected with my own being, something that tells me something about myself because the outer event combined with my inner experience is expressing something unique, the beginning of a hint of my own reality, the reality in which I am living.'

If we want to learn something from this, it would be a good idea to ask ourselves why this event should have been arranged in a way that enables an aspect of our destiny to take place, for the event has been put together in such a brilliant manner that to talk of a coincidence would be no more than idle chatter: 'A higher intelligence must have been involved in bringing about an event at this particular moment, in this location, involving these particular people, at this very moment in my biography when I am wrestling with this particular life question or when I find myself in this particular psychological state.' We realize that serious contemplation of this seemingly superficial event is beginning to make it speak to us. It becomes a destiny event that speaks to us in a language we must learn to understand because it is telling us something about ourselves. With this our new self-knowledge begins.

Initially it is better to choose quite simple, concrete events that are easily described. Supersensible experiences, childhood experiences or emotionally undigested events are not so suitable as starting points. We soon discover that destiny plays a part even in the most ordinary of events. The first step, as well as all the others, should be carried out as accurately as possible.

Describing the event

Describe as accurately as possible every sensory observation you made during the event. For example:

a) What was the exact sequence? How were the scenes arranged? Where were different people standing or moving about? Were any objects involved? Who spoke,

how loudly and in what tone of voice? What clothes were people wearing, what colours or shades were there, what was the weather like? And so on.
b) What happened shortly before and after the event?
c) What did you think and feel during the event? Describe your inner observations in connection with the outer sequence of happenings as accurately as possible.
d) What will impulses were aroused?
e) Now bring your outer and inner observations together in such a way that a characteristic gesture, attitude or way of behaving emerges.

This last task is often the most difficult because we are trying to express a qualitative process by means of a picture. If we find we cannot immediately hit upon such a picture, it might be a good idea to leave this step and wait to see whether our night-time learning can help us come up with a suitable picture next day. There are some specific exercises that can also help here.

2. Collaboration in a group
When we embark on this learning path for the first time it is essential to be accompanied by an experienced facilitator, since the process must be conducted as accurately as possible.

The facilitator will demonstrate how the group can best work together and ensure that the sequence runs smoothly.

3. Hindrances to the learning process
In the description of the event in the first step, as in the subsequent ones, the following blockages can arise:

a) Being unable to observe the external process properly;
b) Therefore also being unable to view the inner observations with sufficient objectivity;
c) Being insufficiently able to distinguish between inner and outer experiences;
d) Having problems with our memory. This is the most dif-

ficult blockage. We have already interpreted and evaluated many of the events in our past, and we therefore tend to mix explanation or evaluation with what actually happened at the time; the feelings and explanations we now have about the event also colour our description.

Blockages a), b) and c) are regularly addressed and corrected during adult learning, so they should not pose too much of a problem. As regards the earlier points c) and d) listed in connection with describing the event, what must be remembered are the thoughts, feelings and impulses of will that arose at the time of the event, not what comes up in us as we try to describe it now. This presupposes an ability to view things very objectively and accurately, which is essential for any self-knowledge we are striving to acquire.

4. Helpful exercises
There are many exercises that can help us overcome our resistance to learning. Some particularly important ones are described below:

A. Reviewing the day backwards every evening is an exercise that is often described in the context of spiritual science. Doing this regularly strengthens our inner confidence and creates a general base for Destiny Learning. It teaches us to stand back from external events, which is essential for every aspect of destiny knowledge.
B. Rudolf Steiner's book *Reincarnation and Karma*[1] refers to a number of exercises that can help to school our eye for memories that are connected with destiny, in contrast to memories that are merely thoughts.

If we find we have too much resistance to working our way through the five stages of Learning Step I, it is perfectly possible to embark on this with the help of an experienced facilitator. Learning Step I and the other six can be tackled in Destiny Learning seminars in which approximately five participants and an experienced facilitator go through all seven

Learning Steps. The work is supported by lectures, artistic activities and specially worked out observation exercises. The participants give each other mutual support, which has proved to be very beneficial for this learning process. It is rare for someone to need the extra help of a counsellor, but this is sometimes necessary in connection with very difficult destiny events. (This book will not discuss counselling in more detail, since it deals here with Destiny Learning for adults in a general way, and not with destiny therapy.)

In what follows, the process of Destiny Learning is described in the way that it has been taught in seminars where it has proved its validity. What we are presenting is a kind of prototype of Destiny Learning seminars since this enables us to describe the basic learning process.

In concluding this section, let us once more remember that those working through destiny events in the manner here described will have to ask themselves how such events can come to be orchestrated in a way that makes them happen at precisely this location, at this particular time and with these particular participants and circumstances. No ordinary understanding would be able to arrange things in a way that enables us to experience exactly what we must experience in order to proceed in our lives. Only a higher being would be capable of doing this, so we now begin to have a presentiment of how powers of destiny shape our lives. This experience can accompany us throughout the following six Learning Steps.

Learning Step II

1. Uniting the destiny event with one's biography
The fifth task e), in Learning Step I, also brings us to the beginning of Learning Step II. The first step is like a destiny breath breathed in from outside and breathed out from inside, but in the characteristic way that 'I myself breathe in and out'. It stands out there alone in an event that appears in our consciousness as a process in space. If we want to internalize this it must unite with our warmth organism, just as in normal learning 'warming to a subject' involves uniting with

Destiny is the Reality in Which We Live 77

it personally. To unite with something personally in Destiny Learning signifies linking it with one's biography. Every individual's life story is unique; it differs from all others, and with it, in the course of time, our ego inscribes itself into the life of the earth. It is a living script, a biographical warmth process. To unite the destiny event with one's biography involves learning to read that characteristic gesture, discovered in task e), as one letter in the script of one's life. Thus a spatial event is united with a temporal process.

How can we learn to do this? The destiny event stood there as an isolated phenomenon which we observed as a spectator. Now, though, the phenomenon is becoming a symptom, a symptom of one's own life history. It is beginning to speak. The spectator is becoming a participant. We have looked at destiny; now destiny comes alive, and life begins to speak our destiny.

This is the basic attitude, but what about the learning process?

We investigate our biography in detail and try to find events in which our behaviour was similar to our behaviour in the event we chose to describe. External circumstances and inner aspects may be entirely different, but qualitatively the gesture shows similar characteristics.

Throughout life we are bombarded with impressions most of which we forget immediately or indeed do not even notice in the first place. But some impressions remain with us, for example a sentence we have read or heard, a mood that accompanied a specific situation, a picture that crops up repeatedly. These are impressions that cannot be explained solely as being part of the relevant circumstances, for the circumstances are merely what causes them to remain in our awareness while others fade.

It is helpful to seek out impressions of this kind in order to discover what the right symptoms are. Three or four such symptoms as examples often suffice to help us recognize our destiny event as something living. This 'living something' is revealed as a symptom, a characterization, of our being. It is a characteristic of our being. This means we have taken an important step forward in recognizing the reality of our destiny.

This biographical examination often takes the form of a kind of self-evaluation in which it is easy to deceive oneself. The examples discovered are often quite similar outwardly but entirely different inwardly. It is therefore important to investigate the similarity and dissimilarity of each example in order to find out whether the observable symptom really has the same gesture in the background or whether it points to something altogether different. It is exceedingly tempting to delve into something much more interesting in one's biography, but if we do this we lose sight of the starting point of the event and soon find ourselves floating in biographical interpretations. So, enough said in respect of holding on to the symptomatic similarity of the chosen examples.

The links between the separate symptoms can be regarded as a thread of continuity running through the whole of one's biography. Having discovered such a thread it is important to realize that it can metamorphose during the course of one's life, especially when it turns out to be one of our life's themes. It is likely to have appeared in our youth in a rudimentary form that hinted at the problem. In middle life it becomes more differentiated, has various aspects and is often more dramatic. In the third period of life, after one's 42nd year, it will probably show itself for what it really is. It has always been present, but only reveals its essential nature much later.

A different angle is presented by an event that appears to be a one-off instance with nothing like it having occurred previously. It is easy to believe that this must therefore have something to do only with our future destiny. However, all destiny is connected to the future; by the very way we deal with it we are creating future destiny. Nevertheless, it is also always connected with the past in some way.

Finally there are events that concern us alone and do not involve anyone else. Even a shared event such as a natural catastrophe or a plane crash is experienced differently by everyone involved, with each individual responding differently too.

The emphasis or meaning of an event can lie more in the past or in the future, as we shall have to discover in Learning

Step III. But there is always some link with our biography. Destiny weaves in time; it is the golden thread running through our development, indeed through the whole evolution of humanity.

A final error can lie in interpreting the examples we have found on the basis of other events within our biography. There is a considerable tendency to do this since it appears a perfectly logical thing to do. Our behaviour then seems to have been caused by all kinds of things that have influenced us during the course of this life. Our present biography, however, supplies us with pictures of our destiny, not of the causes of our destiny, since these lie in our former incarnations and in what happened to us during our spiritual life between our previous death and present birth. We shall return to this in the next section since the temptation to interpret and find psychological reasons is much stronger in the step to be described there.

2. Working together

Let us now imagine the five participants in a seminar situation wanting to proceed together along the path of Learning Step II, 'Uniting the destiny event with one's biography'.

Each participant has meanwhile investigated when and how three or four similar examples of 'his' or 'her' destiny events took place. The group look at the examples together, trying hard to listen to and read the symptoms in the examples until the essential characteristic of each one's destiny appears, takes shape and becomes a being. Much is corrected and made more objective. A mutual learning process takes place, supported and guided by the facilitator. The participants must learn to respect the unique nature of each destiny; they must not generalize or project anything into what is said; they must listen to catch what is essential in the other's words. In this way they support the learning process of each participant and learn how to do this.

At the end of Learning Step II the participants endeavour to give a temporary name to the figure they have discovered, who has emerged and become a living being as a result of their mutual investigation of a few events. Here are some examples:

The Vain Penitent	The Trail-Blazer
The Eternal Refusenik	His Eminence
The Subordinate	The Nice Girl
The Fighter Against Injustice	The Eternal Boy
The Judge	The Missionary
The Gambler	The Nun
The Magician	The Pasha

This naming merely helps the participants to observe in more detail the figure who has emerged. The name is only temporary and is usually corrected or differentiated next day by the participant concerned. The names are merely pictures serving as aids to the learning process. They must not become fixed. At best they reveal only a partial aspect of the real person and can serve as aids for self-knowledge only to the degree that this is supportive at this stage.

3. Supervising the learning process
We have reached a point at which it will be helpful to list some of the fundamental principles to be observed by the facilitator to ensure that this process remains a process of adult learning and does not deteriorate into speculation, belief, blind acceptance and so on. It must remain a process of absolutely independent adult learning.

a) The participant who has told the story of his destiny event remains the only person who decides whether what the others say is right or wrong, whether it does or does not fit the situation. Whatever the others maintain or claim to see, the teller of the event remains responsible for his own learning process; so any attempt to suggest or influence the person must be avoided. The other participants try to observe and think along with the teller, and to provide helpful material, but the teller is the one who assesses the validity of everything.

Destiny is the Reality in Which We Live 81

b) Whatever is found or discovered is initially treated as mere opinion or partial truth only, until other observations and events corroborate it, correct it or show it to be false. After all, we have so far dealt only with a *single* destiny event. Only a *single* thread of continuity has thus far been followed through our biography. A subsequent learning process utilizing another destiny event will probably show up a different gesture, other symptoms, a new thread of continuity. Karma is very complicated and contains many threads that weave hither and thither, crossing and recrossing one another. They may stem from several former incarnations. The first destiny learning process we embark on deals only with isolated aspects of one destiny event.

4. Overcoming the main blockages and hindrances

We hinted in our introduction at various dangers that can arise in this Learning Step. The following characteristics will be needed in order to deal with them:

a) The ability to see one's biography as a picture language rather than merely an accumulation of unconnected facts;
b) The ability to observe symptomatically, and not only phenomenologically or analytically;
c) The ability to differentiate qualitatively between biographical elements, instead of generalizing everything and ascribing it all to some common denominator;
d) When thinking of a name for the being who has emerged one must think synthetically.

There is a useful exercise cited by Rudolf Steiner which can help to strengthen these characteristics.[2] In this exercise we practise making biographical memory pictures transparent in order to discover the powers of destiny at work behind them.

Any exercise is helpful if it teaches us to speak in pictures and study biographies in ways that will show us the symptoms visible in them.

Learning Step III

1. Finding the causes and discovering the learning task they contain

Step III in Destiny Learning is a kind of watershed in that now the time has come to observe the forces of karma, understand them and recognize what they mean. To do this we have to develop an entirely new way of thinking, one that can do justice to the reality of destiny. We shall call it 'heart-thinking', for the heart knows much which the head cannot comprehend.

Steps III, IV and V in the Destiny Learning process show the essence of the karma work we are discussing here; they call for thinking, feeling and will qualities that are different from those applicable in our everyday life. Steps I and II are by way of preparation, while Steps VI and VII create new capabilities: the ability to observe the web of destiny (Step VI) and to apply newly-acquired capabilities in daily life (Step VII). Developing these is the aim of the Destiny Learning processes.

'Nourishing' is the third organic life process in which digestive processes constitute the main item. The same applies in Destiny Learning. Our destiny nourishes us only if we digest it properly; if we do not it creates psychological hindrances. The inevitable consequence of an unfinished destiny task, for example, is being unable to let go: we are carrying undigested destiny around with us. The ability to forget results from working through and digesting destiny in a healthy way. Soul hygiene involves being remorselessly honest in the face of destiny. We need such honesty if we are to lead our life consciously in a way that enables us to develop. Adult learners who want to take charge of their own development must be capable of seeing both why their destiny is as it is and what learning task is hidden in it for the future. Hence our heading for Step III of the Destiny Learning process: 'Finding the cause and discovering the learning task it contains.'

If we are to live, we must nourish our body, but if we fail to digest the food properly we will fall ill. Digestion transforms the elements of our food into something that can be incorporated into our organism and thus made human. This image applies to the next three steps of Destiny Learning, which must be accomplished actively by our ego itself.

2. Finding the causes
This step is, in essence, looking through what has been perceived in the first two steps to what lies behind it. You begin to cross a threshold to touch the 'force field' of karma. There can be no formula for how to do this as it must be read anew out of each situation. Within the phenomena the evidence has presented itself and provided keys for how to look. We only see as far as we are ready and able to see, given the background of experience and development each of us carries at any point in time. Nevertheless our capacity to 'read' qualities and gestures is already greater than we realize. The way is often helped by the kind of questions we ask. Karma questions can be radically different from the logic of everyday life. The answer does not come from this life but by a leap of imagination, to an earlier lifetime. If this source is revealed, the teller themselves will recognise it, because deep in our being lives our past, and we ourselves know—not in our mind but in our heart. We are it!

A stubborn learning blockage immediately confronts us here. Our way of dealing with life as it is now is determined by our everyday consciousness with all its concepts, ideas, memories, interpretations of feelings and the actions we derive from these. Yet this very consciousness is totally unsuited, or indeed confusing, when it comes to discovering and establishing the causes of destiny events. Our ordinary day-time consciousness is unaware of destiny, since the causes of our deeper feelings must be sought in the period before our birth, and those of our impulses of will in former lives. This is the reason why our legs carry us towards the very destiny situations that belong to us. During such a destiny situation we behave 'typically' in a manner unique to ourselves, rather than logically or sensibly. Forces of destiny from the past are at work in our present life; they are the reality in which, all unawares, we live today.

Can we learn to recognize this reality and bear it in our consciousness? We can, but only with our 'heart-thinking', not with our intellectual logic.

The scale of this intellectual blockage and the extent to which we recoil from learning from destiny becomes obvious when we look at all the interpretations we put on our actions in life: the causes stem from our parents, from circumstances, from heredity, from our up-bringing, and so on. We do not realize clearly enough that rather than being its causes, all these things are opportunities enabling us to fulfil our destiny. Our biography can offer explanations for everything, but this does not explain why 'I and I alone' have to get through this particular unique destiny.

Our biography is a picture of our destiny, but in order to find the forces that have created this picture we have to look back into past lives. Powers of karma are hidden in the depths of our being; they work as intuitions in our will and also in what comes to meet us from outside. Our biography is an imaginative picture of this. So Step III begins with the question: Why? 'Why does this living being I discovered at the end of Step II live within me? Where and how did it come into existence?'

3. Discovering the learning task

The second question to be asked in Learning Step III concerns the reason for a destiny event: What is the learning task involved?

This question needs to be asked because wrestling to overcome our weaknesses and inadequacies leads to specific capabilities that cannot be developed in any other way. The capabilities with which we have been born, meanwhile, stem from karmic achievements in earlier lives. Our destiny is a wonderful composition and proves to be a path of self-knowledge if past events are rightly recognized as causes and tasks (Learning Step III), if they are then accepted (Learning Step IV), and lead to learning through practice in everyday life. This path of development can come about if it is trodden as a path of adult learning. Life itself offers us possibilities to develop and learn if we recognize these for what they are, by learning to accept and answer them. In this Learning Step it is important always to establish a balance between cause and task.

The transition from Learning Step II to Learning Step III must be accompanied by a special mode of schooling our relationship to destiny. It must be followed through with great care so that Step III can be conducted properly.

We shall describe one possibility of carrying this out in a group of four to five persons with an experienced facilitator. What can be done obviously depends in each case on the participants and on the facilitator's capabilities.

4. Working together

One participant offers to begin working on the 'whys and wherefores' of his destiny. Allowing plenty of time, Steps I and II are repeated while the other participants listen as they carry within them the two questions 'Why?' and 'What for?' What should be the manner of their listening? Not so much phenomenological or symptomatic, but rather a sensing, feeling, questioning attitude that creates an open space in which something can appear. In doing this the participants go through three stages.

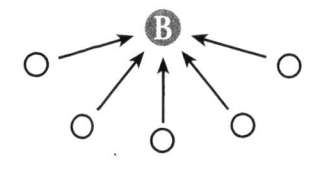

They begin by feeling their way carefully with questions as to what a former life must have been like to bring about causes for today's life situation. The participant in question listens in a particular way, not with his intellect as we do nowadays, passing judgement inwardly on what we hear. He listens in a way that enables him to feel whether any of the possibilities mentioned stir something in him, whether he feels he is the one being talked about, whether the feelings of his heart are touched. It is rather rare for this to happen immediately. More often there has to be a slow and gentle circling by means of brief contributions by the others. The participant states which contribution touches him more, and which less or not at all. This continues until a link between 'then' and 'now' is experienced. It is not easy to describe this instant of recognition in writing without being able to draw on a direct observation. Sometimes a spontaneous 'Yes' is uttered, or a quiet 'Thanks'. Some have a sense of tremendous relief, others are moved, and others have an inkling of some great task facing them. It is remarkable how certain the respondent is in confirming or denying a connection.

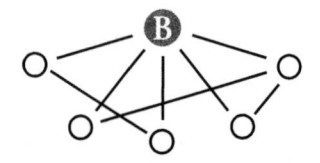

The next stage is to work on what has been discovered in brief conversations, comparing it with the biographical examples that have been given or with the destiny event as it has been described. The learning task often begins to reveal itself while this is going on. The participant in question adds facts from his life that either confirm or contradict the possibility that is emerging. But be careful not to stray into generalities or unimportant side issues! This would interrupt or even destroy the learning possibilities of the process.

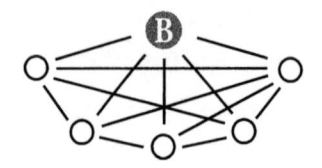

Finally all the participants in this small group inwardly approach the destiny web of the person in question and the being that has become visible in it. They now observe a being, not isolated aspects or possibilities. By doing this they make the original destiny event transparent in all its details. The karmic being, the karmic human being in us becomes visible. Sometimes this is called one's 'second person' or one's 'double'.

Occasionally several former incarnations work into a single destiny event. This makes everything rather more complicated for all the participants, and they will need an acute faculty of discrimination.

These three stages might be termed:

1. Making contact.
2. Discovering details.
3. Observing the 'being'.

Discovering karmic links often brings about a feeling of liberation. If you find the karmic cause, the learning task of your life suddenly becomes obvious. People describe working with others like this as a strong experience of mutual humanity, especially if everyone has a turn in the centre of attention. Many participants have expressed a sense of it being a path to a new feeling of brotherhood. Working together at discovering the profound differences between the participants creates new bonds.

Cooperation in karma work must be learnt and needs practice, and the participants have to adopt a specific attitude. A free unconditional and open space must arise among them and they have to learn how to handle this. It is necessary to set aside all habits of discussion, argumentation, projection, wanting to convince or force one's opinion on others or make assertions. Questions must be aimed at opening up this free space, not closing it or covering it up with unexpressed inherent judgements. Karma is present in the person in question, it is present in the space that has been made, and the participants should learn to observe it. Frequently they are their own worst enemy. Our intellect knows nothing of karma, but all the more can our feeling heart sense it.

A facilitator will have practised this basic attitude and can make it visible; the other members of the group can learn from this and adopt the same attitude themselves. Working together often takes a while to get going, but the participants frequently learn rapidly. After a few days the facilitator more and more becomes just one of the group, joining them in their journey of schooling their sense of karma.

This process takes a while and should not be subjected to time pressures. Four to five people plus the facilitator need about 5 days to reach Learning Step IV together and go on to the beginning of Learning Step V. Usually there is a follow-up dedicated to working with Steps V–VII.

5. Possible karmic causes in former lives
Every human being has been formed in earlier lives by several disparate layers of a very extensive, differentiated and varied range of karmic backgrounds, so it is impossible to compile a list of items to search for. Guidance can be sought in the detailed literature offered by spiritual science on the karmic links between cause and effect in a sequence of lives.[3] Well-researched historical novels and stories describing former cultures can also help us fill the gaps in our often all too inadequate familiarity with earlier times. A few directions are described below, but let us not forget that the main point of departure is always the sensitive observation of the individual in question.

1. What geographical conditions are hinted at by the characteristics we have discovered about the 'karmic being' we are researching? Is there the hot, dry heat of the desert or are there people hunting in the wide open spaces of the steppes? Is there a lot of water with great lakes, lagoons and islands, or is it a mountainous region? Are there caves, stretches of flat country, volcanic hills or the narrow streets of little towns? Which of the elements of earth, water, air or fire was predominant? What kinds of etheric qualities set the scene? (This is particularly relevant in Asia: for instance the 'light ether' in Russia, the 'chemical ether' in China, the 'life ether' in India etc.)

2. What lifestyle do the characteristics of the 'karmic being' hint at? How do the lifestyles of bushmen or nomads, native

Indians, Germanic tribes, the Chinese or the Lapps differ, quite apart from the cultural diversity in the Near East or India? Conclusions about this can be drawn from the way people decorate their home, shape their family life or set up their workplace.

3. Which specific forms of initiation are mirrored in the present characteristics of the 'karmic being'? Mystery centres differed greatly in East, West, North and South—as is still the case today. There were all kinds of composite forms, and over the past two thousand years many have developed decadent traits. It is not surprising that such varied elements are having effects in today's spiritual experiences, or are generating in people a desire for ancient rites. Most of us are quite unaware of the extent to which our convictions and attitudes to life derive from many different principles of ancient initiation. Even just gaining an inkling of the spiritual stream we—or those we meet—have been connected with in earlier lives can have a liberating effect and help increase our understanding and acceptance of differences.

4. We do not know all that much today about the kind of societies people lived in long ago, but the forces that formed those societies live on in us today. Pointers to the type of society or community people have experienced in past lives can be derived from the importance they attach to the different elements in their group of colleagues now. Is it loyalty to the spirit of their group, colleagueship, the structure, the power structure, the main spiritual principles of the group, that matters most to them? The various Christian monastic orders had entirely different rules, each of which provided the monks and nuns with profound religious experiences. Every order cultivated different characteristics of soul and spirit. When people unconsciously bring the rules of an order they have belonged to into a present-day community, this alone can lead to serious conflict and mutual recrimination. The orders of knighthood—King Arthur's Round Table, the Knights of the Grail, the Teutonic Order, the Templars— each had different ideals and aims. Recognizing them liber-

ates us from old bondages and opens up an understanding for social forms that are relevant today.

5. In the above we have looked only at European history. A whole new set of viewpoints on the attitudes and structures of communities would come to light if we were to study the Indian tribes of North and South America, or the past forms of orders, religions and sects in Asia, e.g. Japan, China, Tibetan monasteries, India, Pakistan, or the Near East. Any one of these might have formed our own karmic heritage. Having expanded our horizon in this way we should not be surprised to find amongst our colleagues a former Dervish, a Benedictine monk or nun, an Indian Brahman or an African medicine man.

Once Destiny Learning has helped us discover our own preferred social values as well as those of the others in our group we shall find that a fresh atmosphere of spiritual tolerance arises in which new social forms suitable for the present time can be found. The moment we recognize the old forces that have formed us we can liberate ourselves from them and move on to greater freedom of action. This is the aim of this learning path which enables us—when we have reached Learning Step VII—consciously and creatively to bring a new order into our destiny.

6. Although the capabilities we have acquired in a particular life, through learning and practising a specific calling, are often metamorphosed during the life between death and a new birth, the fundamental attitude nevertheless continues to work on in our will and in our physical bearing. There are differences depending on whether we were a soldier, a peasant, a nun, a housewife, a priestess, a missionary, a clergyman, a troubadour, a counsellor, a craftsman, a scholar, a nurse or anything else in our last life. One can learn to hear whether a 'missionary to the Red Indians' is talking to his wife about the true faith, whether a 'troubadour' is speaking about love, or a 'nun' about morality.

This in no way exhausts the list of possibilities, but these examples will perhaps suffice as a means of stimulating the imagination in trying to fathom the boundless variety of our karmic heritage.

6. The most intractable learning blockages
The logic of karma and the logic of everyday psychology

The most intractable learning blockage of all has already been mentioned. It is our everyday intellect that interprets everything in terms of cause and effect. This is all very well in daily life, but it is unsuitable for Destiny Learning because here cause and effect are related in a different way. To overcome this blockage we need 'heart-thinking', or the 'logic of karma'. How this can be developed will be described below. No lack of respect for psychology or the 'logic of psychology' is intended here, for this discipline is itself now presented with a threshold at which entirely new questions are arising. All we object to is the way certain 'short-circuits' are assumed to provide valid explanations for a person's behaviour when in fact they provide no enlightenment at all as to the 'why' and 'wherefore' of our deeds and opinions.

Moral self-judgement

As the causes of some present characteristics begin to shimmer through, we tend to evaluate them in accordance with today's moral yardsticks, finding them either tremendously virtuous or—especially when they concern ourselves—sinful, despicable or evil. But by projecting today's morality on to our behaviour in a former life we can generate devastating disturbances in the objective process of Destiny Learning because we fail to take into account that with their different attitudes of soul, different religious laws, different duties and power structures, the cultures of other ages cannot be compared with the cultural conditions prevailing in our own time. Human sacrifices, or perhaps burning heretics at the stake, were duties imposed by religion that could not always be evaded—or indeed perhaps we belonged among those heretics. Or perhaps we were involved in tribal warfare in Africa at a time when the enemy had to be exterminated if our own tribe was to survive. Even in fairly recent incarnations there will have been remarkable mixtures of necessity and atrocity. In our life between death and the next birth, beings of the hierarchies show us and let us experience the true cause of our deeds, thereby awakening in us the impulse to compensate for past deeds in the coming life. If we measure the karmic truth against present-day yardsticks we are likely to burden it with heavy feelings of guilt. By doing this we either cover it up or paralyse our will and fail to tackle the actual transformative task of Destiny Learning. Unconscious self-punishment for old karma which we do not clearly understand is an all too frequent phenomenon. When several people are working on this together, the facilitator must ensure that the participants handle their moral self-evaluation in a healthy and objective way. It is better to speak of mistakes, illusions or one-sidedness than to brand people's actions as 'sins', condemning ourselves or others because of them.

Two kinds of karmic blockage

We need to distinguish between two kinds of undigested old karma, both of which can occur. They are diametrically opposed. The 'karmic beings' discovered during Learning Steps II and III with their characteristic traits (see the many examples given) can be of two opposite types and we must distinguish between them. They come into existence as a consequence of our failure to transform our destiny task.

The first type is connected with illusions we have about ourselves, a self-image to which we cling. In this case we feel we are very special people with a very special mission, often accompanied by the gift of clairvoyance. This illusory self-image then colours everything around us, and we imagine our clairvoyant experiences to be true revelations. We fail to realize that the only thing revealed to us is our own self-love. Our vanity appears to be a beneficial being of light, while our artistic gifts bear the mark of genius. Often there are also moral illusions: 'I have forgiven everyone so I have no problems with my fellow human beings.' Love of self and love of Christ are frequently confused. This euphoria about ourselves, this ego trip, has of course as many faces as there are self-illusions. (Such illusions are contributory elements in the formation of almost every sect.) 'Karmic beings' of this kind have the effect of estranging us increasingly from reality, causing us to live on our own spiritual island and thus fail to take objective account of our destiny—which is also something spiritual—so that Destiny Learning cannot show us our real learning task. Other side effects are an increasing blindness towards the needs and ills of others in the world, and also a tendency to lead a chaotic life in a blissful feeling of being able to rise above everything.

The second type of 'karmic being' is expressed not by a floating consciousness but by a hardening element in one's soul, making it difficult to let go of certain concepts, ideas, feelings and ways of behaving which remain as though stuck inside us. We languish in a self-made prison, unable to escape and suffering as a result. Fear of karmic reality lives in this being, often reinforced by feelings of guilt.

The one type of being causes us to flee into other worlds to escape the demands of our destiny, while the other shackles us to the earthly world by means of the fear we feel concerning the demands of destiny. Both types can block Destiny Learning, but they do so in very disparate ways. Self-love leads to illusions about oneself while fear generates a hardening within oneself.

Our experience of these destiny blockages is as divergent as the 'karmic beings' themselves. In the first type we experience bliss, in the second we become isolated. So dealing with them calls for different approaches. Working in a group, the facilitator as well as the participants must learn to handle the two in different ways. A participant who manifests the first type of being will need to be surrounded by much warmth and love, for letting go of an illusory image of oneself brings about an emptiness that can lead to depression. So such a person needs good friends. In the case of a being leading to fear and isolation, the person will need encouragement and genuine trust in daring to move away from the prison he has built for himself.

Although only briefly and inadequately, we have sketched both types of 'karmic being' to help readers differentiate between them and continue the search on their own.

Having discovered the causes for one of the two types of being, the learning task to be tackled is to create a balance between the two. We all tend to have both types in us, although one of the two is dominant, but at the same time we also strive to find a healthy balance between the two extremes. Destiny Learning can thus become a never-ending learning for life which we can accept as a way of ever again achieving balance between our one-sided tendencies. In doing this we are preparing for Learning Step IV.

Pre-judging karmic interpretations

It is very difficult to be unbiased in treading a path of self-discovery in Destiny Learning if we already 'know', perhaps even by name, who we were in our last life or indeed in several former incarnations, and also if we 'know' what our future destiny holds in store. It is irrelevant whether someone else has told us or whether we have found it out through clairvoyance, regression, under hypnosis or whatever. Relevant is whether we have found it through an independent adult learning process.

When working in a group, someone in this situation merely checks the possibilities suggested by the others to see whether they confirm his 'knowledge'. Such a person cannot listen with an open heart, so his learning path is blocked.

Even if our own research has led us to suspect some connections, it is necessary to push this to one side. Every destiny event we examine on this learning path brings with it new aspects, contrasts, even confirmations, for destiny is always many-faceted, very varied and so complicated that all we can do is follow a guiding thread, one particular aspect, of any event. When a further opportunity arises and we bring forward a different destiny event during another Destiny

Learning process, we will often find unexpectedly different answers. We must always remain open to these.

The urge to know everything

If we want to force the issue and learn too much all at once on our path of Destiny Learning, this too can bring about a blockage. Are we really capable of knowing and enduring 'everything' there is to know about our incarnations and karma? Wanting to know everything about oneself and others at any price can easily lead to sensationalism based on unrestrained curiosity which obscures the real purpose of Destiny Learning.

In real life, destiny serves as a means of developing ourselves. It presents us with concrete life facts from which we can learn more and more on our path to self-knowledge; it allows us to learn and understand just as much as we require in order to make the right next step towards the future. Reincarnation provides us with a new chance to develop further. Every destiny event we encounter asks a question that needs to be understood and answered so that it can lead us to make a conscious, well-founded step into the future. The path of Destiny Learning we have been describing here is not founded on unbridled sensationalism and curiosity but provides a very practical, concrete learning activity that is commensurate with the demands life makes on us. If our motives and aims in Destiny Learning are based on this, then we shall find it a support in life; if not, such work can degenerate into pernicious speculation.

Fear of working with karma

One very damaging blockage that is usually unconscious is an inner opposition to any concrete knowledge about destiny. People reveal this attitude in quite innocent remarks they make, and such an attitude prevents active participation in the work. Some such remarks are: 'This is very dangerous!' 'It is pure speculation!' 'You cannot be sure!' 'Such things are only for very highly-developed initiates!' 'There is no need to know anything about karma; it's enough to approach life with a positive attitude!' The author has frequently heard expressions of inner defensiveness and warnings such as these but has always found them to be without foundation and based on an inability to detect the underlying fear. Younger people are less prone to such declarations. There is at present so much speculation about human beings and human relationships that for this reason alone it is a good thing to tackle Destiny Learning as a way of waking up to the realities in life in an objective learning way.

Rudolf Steiner often mentioned the inner opposition he encountered, specifically from individuals striving for spiritual development, as soon as he approached destiny events quoted quite practically and concretely from real life. The cause must be sought in the fear of threshold experiences that can be met with when one comes face to face with destiny.

7. Measures to protect the learning process

1. Even when several people join forces to work on it together and support one another, Destiny Learning must remain an individual, independent adult learning process. Each participant takes responsibility for him or herself. This is how those in the learning process can be protected. The facilitator, being more experienced, must make sure that the separate learning steps are kept tidily apart and that the transition between them is carried out correctly and consciously. This applies to all the steps but is especially important with regard to Learning Step III in which one begins to approach former incarnations and the work that takes place on them during the life between death and the next birth.
2. A second protection is given by the rule that only the person in question may decide whether something does or does not apply; that person alone must bear the responsibility for this. There must be no self-delusion, and the participant must not allow himself to be influenced by any of the others. He alone is the one to decide whether something is true or false. The facilitator must be especially vigilant about this.

3. A third protection lies in keeping an open mind about any cause one might discover, always having at the back of one's mind the thought: 'This might be the case, but the situation might also have been quite different.' In Learning Step V, when the time comes to practise in everyday life, we frequently discover entirely new traits in the 'karmic being' we have found within ourselves, and can then readjust our findings.
4. As a fourth protection one must ask how far or how deeply one should probe. When several participants are working together, they should check regularly to see whether they have gone far enough to achieve what can be achieved. The individual must decide when something has become sufficiently clear to him or whether there is something missing which he would still like to explore with the help of the others. Our usual attitude of being obsessed by success and perfection is inappropriate here. When Steps I, II and III have been accomplished properly in the form of a learning process, the participants gain a deep sense of satisfaction and enthusiasm at having found through their mutual endeavour something they regard as extremely important.
5. Another protection arises through working together, since those involved become more skillful at Destiny Learning as they progress from one participant to the next. The group members each explore, correct and adjust each other, thus step by step reaching a common understanding. If the facilitator himself also tells of a destiny event and the group sets out to help him search for the cause and task it contains, the collaboration gets better and better.

8. Supportive activities for Learning Step III

Rudolf Steiner has described the laws of karma and reincarnation and also the experiences of the soul between death and the next birth in a number of written works and lectures. He has also given numerous descriptions of karmic connections using individual biographies as examples, and has explained the various different types of the being we call the 'double' or our 'karmic being'. We should gradually familiarize ourselves with all these things in connection with Learning Step III of Destiny Learning. The 'four-days-three-nights' karma exercise can also be a great help in finding causes in earlier lives for today's destiny in Learning Step III and in combination with the other Learning Steps.[4]

Selected painting exercises co-ordinated to suit the learning path have proved very helpful in finding the hidden 'karmic being' that is the cause of destiny events in our present life.

When handled correctly, interpreting the causes can in itself have a healing effect in that what happens to us is no longer hidden in darkness while we try to feel our way towards its meaning. The 'whys' and the 'wherefores' are no longer pushed aside through our desire to explain everything by declaring some events in our destiny to be meaningless or a coincidence, by attributing them to external circumstances, or by making those around us responsible for our happiness or unhappiness. Getting to know the true causes helps us re-evaluate all our values. We no longer use our surroundings and circumstances as excuses and reproaches about the course of our lives. Instead everything then gains a much deeper meaning as we experience universal fairness and meaningful harmony in the universe.

We now have a different assessment for the destiny event brought forward in Step I. It is more objective, and our task for the future is getting clearer. Every subsequent destiny encounter appears in a new light, as a compensation for the past or a redemptive task for the future, as a possibility for renewal or a preparation for future steps, and so on.[5]

Learning Step IV

Wählt ich nicht seit Ewigkeiten
alle meine Schicksale selbst?
Alles, was geschieht, will ich.

Did not I ever choose
All my destinies myself?
Whatever happens: I will it.

Novalis

1. Accepting one's destiny

Learning Step IV poses a riddle in the formulation 'Accepting one's destiny'. What is it we are supposed to accept? During the course of the first three Learning Steps we have discovered one single aspect of our destiny, and no more. This aspect was depicted as a living being, a hitherto hidden part of our own human being. As we proceed along our own learning path this being is revealed to us as we accomplish the first three Learning Steps. We are then able to give a temporary name to this being who has some specific characteristics, a name that describes these characteristics. We can glimpse the causes linking this being to us from former incarnations as well as the metamorphosis it went through between the last death and present rebirth. We can also sense the question it is setting us for the future.

It is of course perfectly possible to encounter this being—and more than once—in circumstances other than those discussed on the learning path described in this book. This part of our being has been given many names: the shadow, the double, the sub-personality, 'my other being', 'my second being', and so on. In the present context we are treating this being as an effect of former destiny appearing in us in this life as a second, hitherto unknown person. Since this being can be experienced in a profusion of different guises, any name we give it must be seen as a diminution of reality. We shall therefore term it our 'karmic being' without wanting to fix it in any way.

To pursue a further step, Step IV, in Destiny Learning involves finding and accepting this 'karmic being' within ourselves. By accepting it we individualize it, thus recognizing it as a part of ourselves, as something that belongs to us. But perhaps 'to accept' is too narrow an expression for what is really meant here. It would be more accurate to talk of 'approving' or 'affirming' the karmic being, or of 'confirming one's destiny'.

Our 'higher ego', which has its origin in the wellspring of creation and bears within it all our inadequacies and achievements, our past and our future, reaches far beyond the normal consciousness we have of our self.[6] This more comprehensive being gives us the strength and the creativity we need in order to deal consciously with that 'shadow being' we have discovered in us, accepting and transforming it. Our 'higher ego' supports us as we pursue the path of learning on which we want to transform our weaknesses into new capabilities. In doing this it connects with our everyday ego, growing through it and extending its consciousness of our individuality.

By accepting and concurring with destiny we enable our everyday ego to join forces with our higher ego. Our everyday ego then becomes capable of receiving the prenatal will intentions of our higher being. This strengthens our everyday will. Nothing gives our will more strength than an earnest acceptance of our destiny. Awakening the will is here an existential act.

Full acceptance is only possible if we regard reincarnation and karma as the means, bestowed on us by divine powers, that will enable us to achieve freedom. By grace it is given to us to see and understand a portion of our destiny. In voluntarily accepting the developmental task this portion brings with it we perform a liberating deed. The powers of destiny bestow this possibility on us; it is up to us to seize the opportunity. We must do away with every feeling of original sin, any belief that we are a wicked person who must be punished for our sins. We must not judge and condemn ourselves in this manner.

We must be filled with a positive feeling of joy at being helped to take a step towards freedom. Then we shall lose all our fear and all those feelings of guilt that attack so many people when they experience a part of their double and fail to understand what a grace and what a gift this experience is.

So long as we regard the biblical 'fall' as a punishment from God, accepting our unredeemed shadow must seem tantamount to an avowal of sin. But if we comprehend our destiny as a learning path of the highest order that leads us to independence, self-responsibility, free choice and thus to freedom, deep gratitude arises to take the place of any such avowal. Our path of Destiny Learning can then serve both human and cosmic evolution. We understand that to go through the 'Fall of Man' was a divine intention to make the development of freedom possible. Reincarnation and karma are the means by which this task is accomplished.

The human being must, however, will to tread this learning path if Step IV is to become a free deed opening up the possibility of finding true self-knowledge. This Learning Step is the heart of all three learning paths.

Do not believe that this fourth step, accepting one's destiny, is easy to accomplish. A good many of us have felt sure of having accepted our destiny only to find that this was still only wishful thinking. In Learning Step V, when we begin to practise what we have learnt in everyday life, we soon discover whether we have duped ourselves and decided too easily. Then we shall have to return to Learning Step IV.

It is so easy to say we want to accept our destiny and transform it. But we soon forget the tremendous variety of ways in which our own destiny is linked to that of the people we meet in life. We have to accept not only the shadow being we have ourselves created but also the many justified, partially justified and unjustified actions other people have committed in relation to us. Only when we take all this upon ourselves do we genuinely break with the terrible causality of 'an eye for an eye, a tooth for a tooth'. In the past, blood-feuds and vendettas stood in the way of transforming old destiny into new. Today the same obstacles are created by psychological ways of punishment and judgement. The main emphasis in Learning Step IV is therefore on our own decision to accept our 'double', our 'karmic being', and take upon ourselves what others do to us. In Learning Step V we then endeavour to practise this in everyday life.

Note: In Part Three of this book the professional profile of the adult educator describes him as an enabler for the vocational learning process. In Destiny Learning, though, the adult educator is not so much an enabler as a fellow human being, a friend, since it is the powers of destiny themselves who are the enablers here.

A. *Experiencing the midnight hour*

We know from the literature of spiritual science that in the very middle of the period between a previous death and the next incarnation, when we are entirely oriented towards the macrocosm, we experience a review of all our previous incarnations. At this moment we 'see' how we have become what we are at that moment; and then we have a preview of what a human being can become if he develops everything he is capable of developing freely on the earth. The ideal image of a fully developed human being appears before us, whereupon the will arises in us to embark on a new incarnation, the will to return to earth in order to take the next step in this tremendous process of evolution. This will is spirit-will.

Accepting our destiny in Learning Step IV represents a small yet very essential confirmation of that cosmic will, a confirmation of what happened once before, prior to our birth. This is why accepting our destiny strengthens our earthly will. When we say: 'I myself have willed my destiny,' this is true only of the midnight hour situation between death and rebirth. It can, however, be confirmed as a free decision once we have returned to the earth.

B. *Experiences during sleep*

Less well known is the fact that a similar process takes place every night when we meet our angel who is the guide of our destiny events. During each night our handling of destiny during the day and the consequences of this for the future are assessed. Archangels and archai also play a decisive role in this process. In Learning Step IV, in which we make decisions regarding our destiny during the day, the consequences of these decisions are morally perceived during the night. We have a more conscious encounter with our destiny guide (angel), and this has an effect on the subsequent steps. Nighttime learning gains in importance in Destiny Learning because in our semi-deep sleep we experience the prenatal planetary spheres and in our deep sleep we live backwards through all our previous incarnations right back to the first and beyond.[7]

C. Directing our karma

Accepting our destiny is most fruitful if it creates a balance between acceptance of the past and our intentions for the future. Then we wake up to the present. This is a balancing process, always fluctuating rhythmically.

The balance can be disturbed either by a heavy burden from the past or by some frivolous action with regard to the future, or vice versa. It is widely believed, mistakenly, that we do not need to know about the past if our intentions for the future are entirely good. We can only individualize our karma by constantly seeking to find a mobile balancing point between the two. The image of scales is too reminiscent of judgment and punishment—right versus wrong. We must transform the image of judging into a continuous search for direction. Then we shall find the right direction in which to step forward to a positive, Christian assessment of our destiny. The judgment meted out by the judge is replaced by the finding of our path's right direction.

Each night in the cosmos, together with our angel and our higher self, our astral body becomes the valuer of our human soul in its present truth. And it is our ego that points out the direction for a continuing process of development. Thus acceptance of our destiny in Step IV becomes the creative direction that is to be realized in Step V.

D. Working with the powers of destiny

As we proceed with Destiny Learning we become increasingly aware of the purpose and significance of the work of all the hierarchies and what they do for us. Our decision to accept our destiny can then also mean that we want to work together consciously with the powers of destiny. We understand their labours with the utmost gratitude and set about carrying them further. During the night they become aware of this. On the 'path of spiritual schooling' this is described as the encounter with the lesser Guardian of the Threshold who regularly makes us aware of our web of destiny.

2. Working together in Step IV

Since Learning Step IV is so entirely individual in character the ongoing collaboration among the participants must be focussed even more than before to the possibilities and needs of the participants themselves.

A start is made by recapitulating and rounding off Step III. When meeting again the next day there is frequently an experience of it having been transformed and adjusted by the experiences of the night.

A span of time is needed, half an hour perhaps, in which each participant can ponder *alone*, relive the whole experience and think about how he should deal with the 'karmic being' he has discovered now that he has accepted it.

In conclusion there is a conversation in which no one need say more than he wishes. It can happen that the other participants who have now become our new-found friends can make suggestions that are important for us.

3. Some learning blockages

1. Heart-thinking

Obviously Learning Step IV of Destiny Learning calls for a rather different kind of heart-thinking as compared with Step III. We have to grasp it much more firmly with our will. In addition we have to live through the consequences. Accepting one's destiny does not seem too difficult in theory, but to transform it with the forces of our heart is another matter altogether.

Those who have experienced heavy blows of destiny or who have shared the seemingly hopeless sufferings of others, only realizing years later what noble and wonderful consequences these might have for the future, will not find it easy to accept destiny, even when they have recognized the causes. So they may have to repeat the acceptance process to make it ever more real and existentially true.

2. Our views of good and evil

We carry in us certain out-dated images of good and evil that can work as impediments to a positive acceptance of destiny or the formation of a free decision. Such images are, for example, the attitude of passing judgement on ourselves, with its accompaniment of morally keeping account of our good and bad deeds. Good deeds have to be rewarded, bad ones punished.

In reality, almost everything in our destiny is a mixture of both. Something we describe as evil can lead to a good outcome while something we might call good can end in illusion and self-glorification. The more mistakes we make the more we can learn from them (which does not mean to say that mistakes are praiseworthy). By working our way through our many illusions we strengthen our sense of truth, and our former attitude of judging and condemning has been transformed into an understanding tolerance towards ourselves and others.

To transform destiny into an independent learning process requires us to develop a new and appropriate valuing process.

3. The concept of grace

So long as we regard life as a once-and-for-all event we remain dependent on God's grace for our salvation and redemption. The concept of reincarnation changes this in that karma and reincarnation bestow on our development the element of continuity which allows for the possibility of continual transformation until our aim is reached. Destiny itself then becomes God's grace, with reincarnation being the great gift which makes our continuing existence and our continuous development possible. Religious individuals might experience learning blockages here because of the way the churches have claimed the concept of grace for themselves. Pietro Archiati has discussed this matter in detail in his book *Reincarnation in Modern Life*.[8]

4. Generalization

Making generalizations about how to evaluate human relationships is frequently a source of learning blockages. One example is: 'If there are difficulties, both parties are always to blame.' This obscures the essential aspect regarding one's acceptance of destiny. Even though it may be a partial truth, a generalization like this wipes out reality, since karmically every human relationship is unique and should be seen and accepted as such. Generalizations are the enemy of Destiny Learning.

Learning Step V

1. Practising in daily life

Learning Step V takes place in everyday life. To describe it we can only listen to what people tell us who have endeavoured to deal in a conscious way with their discovered karmic forces and the encounters they experience. A great deal of discipline is needed to tread this path, and on the other hand it is entirely up to the individual how he or she approaches it. An important part of Destiny Learning is making one's own discoveries about suitable ways to act and practise for this part of the learning process. What follows should therefore be seen purely as suggestion and not in any way a set of 'instructions for use' that must be followed to the letter. The first three Learning Steps need to be followed quite strictly, but continuing on from there much greater freedom in discovering and observing has to be practised. Destiny Learning is a path towards an ever more free and creative treatment of our destiny (Learning Step VII), and to achieve this we have to develop the intuitive ability to observe how the powers of karma work.

2. Preparation

Initially we need to realize that the 'karmic being' whom we have meanwhile accepted, and about whose future possibilities we have some inklings, is actually still quite a stranger to us. We now have to get to know 'him' or 'her' a good deal better. Preparation here means getting better acquainted.

Some people regularly set aside a period of free time during which they can converse quietly and inwardly with their 'karmic being'. But if one wants to get to know someone really well one has to find a suitable setting. Our 'karmic being' needs this too, becoming visible to us only if we provide fitting surroundings; and the 'being' actually gives us hints in this respect. A fearful being, for example, needs encouragement; a being full of hate needs positivity and warmth; an arrogant being needs humorous acceptance; and as for a primadonna—well, what does she need in order to feel accepted? Certainly no criticism!

So constant practice is required to make a home for this being we have created, a home in which it can be lovingly received.

Another means of getting to know our 'karmic being' better is to understand its deeds and actions. This requires a good deal of concentration and presence of mind. We live with the question: '*When* do you put in an appearance? What occasions or what conditions rouse you to action? What sense impressions or inner images make me aware of you?' We have to catch the moment when the being appears on the scene, and when we have learnt how to do this we go on to the next question: '*What* is the manner of your appearance?' After a while we begin to know our 'karmic being' better and better. It becomes increasingly palpable and familiar, and we can then almost predict how it will behave towards our surroundings in specific situations. 'Here you are again!' we then say.

These two ways of getting to know the being either inwardly or outwardly can of course also be combined. Both methods call for a great deal of practice, and there is a basic question underlying them both: 'What effect do you, my karmic being, have on the people around me?' A long period of practice will be needed while we strengthen our objectivity and sense of truth before we can reach an honest conclusion about this, and our fellow beings can be a great help to us in this respect.

In Learning Step I we practised how to distinguish accurately between our perception of external happenings and the inner feelings these arouse in us. Now, however, we must find out about our inner stirrings (of which we have thus far been totally unaware) and the effect they have on our surroundings. One 'being' swallows up every shred of sympathy; another is always doing battle; a third turns on the pressure, exerts power, is a control freak; a fourth is a loving father confessor; a fifth never stops expecting the worst; a sixth has an unsatiable appetite for love. The trouble is that we are almost entirely unaware of these effects nowadays. Our life of ideas, our feelings, our intentions and behaviour bear the stamp of today's culture, education and experience. Yet our 'karmic being', which is the result of past lives, is also here with us and every bit as effective. Only when we have truly accepted our 'karmic being' shall we be able to detect the effect it has on others.

One aspect of getting to know it is to observe attentively the effect it has on the way other people behave towards us. Good friends who understand these matters can point such things out to us because they have learnt to observe accurately. One of many fields of practice therefore is to study the effects of 'doubles' with one's good friends. However, these effects also have karmic implications, so that one person will experience them in one way, another quite differently, while a third might not notice them at all.

Once our 'karmic being' has become quite familiar to us we find ourselves getting rather friendly with it. Former fears and illusions, inflexibilities and euphorias caused by it gradually disappear and it becomes a part of our own being, accompanying us always. A transformation can then begin to take place in which it can become a real friend and counsellor, for our 'karmic being' knows the means by which it must be redeemed.

This last sentence requires further clarification. When our 'karmic being' begins to manifest the characteristics of a 'double', in other words when we perceive it as apparently having a human form, it also possesses a biography of its own. It came into being under entirely different circumstances in former incarnations, and thereafter followed its own path of development through karmic sequences of cause and effect in our earlier lives on earth. In our times between death and a new birth it underwent transformation again and again, appearing now as we have come to know it at present. It is therefore relevant to ask what this 'karmic being' is capable of observing. It knows well the threads of destiny that created it, and since we have played our part in spinning them, it is entirely justifiable and meaningful to ask the being: 'What can I do for you?'

Our daily transformation work will increasingly enable us to understand our 'karmic being' and listen to what it wants to tell us. Daily practice will make us aware of the karmic web in which we are situated since any practising we do in our daily life is also connected with our fellow human beings. Up to this point we have been treading our own individual learning path, but now, as we practise, we enter the karmic web of which we are a part. More and more people are becoming aware of the powers of karma, for in the final analysis the whole of humanity is karmically intertwined. In addition to this there is also humanity's karmic connection with earth and cosmos.

Having got to know our 'karmic being' we must continue to practise with it daily, as will be described in the next section.

3. Day-time and night-time learning

Experience has shown that night-time learning makes a considerable contribution towards our daily practice, not only strengthening but also correcting the exercises. The enhancement is especially noticeable if day-time and night-time learning are in harmony.

The reason for this is that each night our higher being, spirit-self or 'genius', also known as our higher ego, evaluates how we have acted during the day in respect of our destiny. The way we have treated our destiny directly determines our future destiny, be it next day, in the near future or in our next life.

This higher ego-being depends for its own development on how our everyday self tackles the requirements of karma. That is why it 'appraises' the extent to which we have accomplished our Destiny Learning process and what kind of consequences are likely to ensue in the future.

Having got to know our 'karmic being' better, we notice that we are increasingly aware of it, that it grows ever more concrete for us, and that our encounters with it are therefore less tense and less burdened by anxiety, so that a little more humour and friendliness can play a part in our conversations with it.

Four questions are important, in particular, and it is a good idea to ask them each evening like a kind of karmic daily review:

1. When, where and how did I encounter my 'karmic being' today?
2. How did it conduct itself during those encounters, and how did it affect those around me?
3. What did I do for and with it?
4. How should I act for it tomorrow?

The first three of these questions are explorative, and if we repeat them daily we shall gain more and more clarity as to how our 'karmic being' behaves in us under specific circumstances. After a few days we can change the first two questions by adding the word 'now'. This will reveal whether there has been any progress.

The fourth question has to be taken with us into the night where we then ask it of our night-time learning. Next morning, frequently at the moment of waking up, sometimes a little later and certainly at our next encounter with our 'karmic being', hints emerge which lead to a deeper understanding, generate unaccustomed feelings and give suggestions for a change in our behaviour. Initially this is somewhat infrequent and unclear, but regular repetition brings it about more frequently and more strongly. Our awareness of the presence of our 'karmic being' increases until we are fully aware of it in everyday situations.

Spiritual science confirms that our higher being, our real ego, which has worked on shaping our karma during the period between death and the next birth, experiences nightly what we have been doing with regard to our karma during the previous day. By asking those three questions regularly we connect with this higher ego of ours, and this can enhance our karmic learning path.

Our angel bears this higher ego within its own being. Its task is to ensure that our karma runs correctly during the daytime. It often needs to adapt the shape of the following day to fit what we have learnt during the previous day because it is during the night that it prepares the events of the coming day. Thus it accompanies our process of Destiny Learning very closely, and we become aware of a gradual change in how outer and inner karmic forces work for and in us. Thus our angel and our higher ego become our allies in day-time and night-time Destiny Learning, and they support the transformation of our 'karmic being'.

4. The dynamic between Learning Steps III, IV and V

We have so far followed only a single thread from that original destiny event up to our daily destiny exercises. In practice a number of threads should and indeed can be followed by taking several destiny events through the whole process. From Learning Step III the threads then begin to intertwine, so that by the time we reach the exercises of Step V our 'karmic being' becomes much clearer and more easy to grasp. As we continue along the learning path the being becomes visible in increasing detail. We discover new elements that point to paths through different incarnations, while a kind of symbiosis takes place between some of the threads.

The fifth organic life process is termed 'maintaining'. In a physical organism the process of 'maintaining' depends to a large extent on the day/night rhythm of life forces being used up through our day-time consciousness and their replenishment during sleep at night. In adult learning this natural rhythm is replaced by the rhythm of regular exercising which helps us retain what we have learnt and move on with it to Learning Step VI in which it is transformed into further capabilities.

Practising involves coming to grips with resistances. In Destiny Learning it is our 'karmic being' that provides the necessary resistance. We maintain it by practising correctly with it, so that we can transform it into a part of our own being which will then appear as a new capability in Learning

Step VI. The resistance provided by our 'karmic being' helps us get to know the powers of karma very well indeed, including the way they work.

Karma exercises also help us develop a new way of 'perceiving': destiny-seeing or destiny-hearing. Initially we learn to apply this to the past, but then we can also use it for present life-situations. In the end it becomes a perception of our karmic web. This is a gradual process that only comes to fruition fully in Learning Step VI. As we practise we first of all notice how something sounds for us in the way a person speaks, not so much in what is said but how it is expressed. This is because the way we speak is an expression of our karma, and this can gradually come to be perceived through Inspiration. That karmic pictures also appear is not a contradiction, since these pictures are usually triggered by what we hear.

By regularly practising new ways of conducting ourselves we also work back on to the earlier Learning Steps, so that we can run through them more and more rapidly. The karmic dimension of a new destiny event is more quickly recognized, as is also its significance in our biography. We are more apt to recognize whether we have discovered a new cause, deriving perhaps from the incarnation before last, and then once again we have to practise acceptance.

Finally, as we continue to practise, the significance of our karmic connections with our fellow human beings becomes more apparent to us, so that we can discern what their karmic questions to us might be.

The more we practise the better at it we become. Then practising no longer calls for stupefying repetition but rather for a creative attitude in every situation. For quite some time now people have longed to develop a social art. But too few realize as yet that this should be learnt via Destiny Learning. We discover this as we carry on practising this path.

There is a degree of mutual reflection between Step III and Step V. What our heart-thinking has discovered by way of a cause and a task (Step III) our practising will must now look at (Step V). We find new causes and the task changes as we proceed; it becomes more real, often more difficult than expected, or else it shifts to a new direction. The act of acceptance has to be renewed regularly. By practising these three learning processes on a regular basis, making them a part of our way of life and learning, the three steps are gradually transformed into a dynamic process and point to the basis and fertile soil of our new awareness of destiny.

The day/night exercise often generates side-effects. From this, too, we learn that Steps III, IV and V are a dynamic whole. In practising Step V, for example, we suddenly realize that we failed to accept properly an essential aspect of the 'double' in Step IV, or that in Step III we only worked on one particular aspect, so that we must now include other incarnations and other 'doubles'. Without knowing the cause we cannot find the solution.

It is also possible that we need to practise some quite different exercises in order to do away with damaging effects on other people. In short: The enhancement achieved through night-time learning brings many things to the surface that have existed for a long time but remained undetected. So do not draw hasty conclusions!

The fifth life process is 'maintaining'. The practising we do in Destiny Learning also serves to 'maintain' something. The effort we make in our daily dealings with the sense-perceptible and supersensible powers of karma is transformed each night into an ability to become increasingly conscious of these forces in everyday life. The growth of this new capability brings us to Learning Step VI, but the intention at this juncture was to point out how even the first and second exercises are connected with the growth of a new capability: becoming acquainted with the karmic being and transforming the karmic being.

We must learn to cultivate Steps III, IV and V as a dynamic process. They are the heart of Destiny Learning. Since we can only discover karmic causes to a limited degree—finding one possibility here, another aspect there—we can never entirely reach the end of the process; it is never finished.

The responsibility of shouldering our karma (Step IV) can take place at various levels. In our life of thoughts and ideas it becomes insight, in our inner life it becomes a far-reaching feeling element as a basic mood, in our will it should become the incentive for our actions. In this sense, too, we never reach a final end, so a constantly renewed karmic spirit-mindfulness is demanded of us.

The rhythmical character of the process in Step V has already been mentioned. This in itself shows that the three stages must move along together in a balanced way. Considerable disturbances can arise if too many causes are recognized and too little daily practising is going on, or when there is too much practising without sufficient recognition of the 'whys and wherefores'. Particularly serious trouble can ensue if we apply karmic interpretations to our fellow human beings when our own ego has not taken full and free responsibility for our own karma (in so far as we have recognized it).

We learn to work with Destiny Learning in a healthy way if we move continuously between the various steps, always re-establishing balance and setting up new polarities from a mid-point, thus following a healthy path of self-knowledge.

Steps III, IV and V, but also indeed all seven Learning Steps, can be seen to play a part in every kind of therapy. In the path towards true self-knowledge under discussion here we work with the powers of karma. Within these lies the reality in which we live. Some might like to call this a therapy, but they would have to agree that it is a 'world therapy' of a kind which the world does indeed desperately need for its further progress.

Practising Step V in everyday life we become directly aware that this has an effect on those around us. In this sense Destiny Learning becomes a social issue. That is why an 'inner hygiene' needs to be learnt as an accompaniment to practising Learning Steps III, IV and V.

There are some quite concrete exercises that serve to transform our web of destiny. Much of this has been discovered and successfully applied in counselling and psychotherapy, too. We shall purposely not list these exercises here since we are talking about an individual Destiny Learning process that requires each individual to work creatively in order to proceed in a manner suited to his or her existing situation.

5. Working together

Since Learning Step V is carried out in everyday life, each participant has to work on his own rather than in the group. Those working daily on their destiny do have a need, though, for a colleague who is following a similar path, with whom they can exchange experiences. The results are very fruitful if this can be arranged. Nevertheless, the main task in Step V is to practise assiduously. Our social surroundings represent our field of action and it is here that we achieve the necessary karmic faculties.

6. Some learning blockages

A. *Forgetting*

Forgetting the resolves reached in Step IV is a common blockage that occurs very frequently. We are much too busy, have no time, no opportunity or inner tranquillity to bother any more with our 'karmic being'. Quite often destiny takes a hand by unexpectedly bringing us face to face with it again. Nevertheless, it is unhealthy not to persevere in following up the insights we have gained. The seven Learning Steps together form a totality, and one should do justice to this.

B. *Superficiality*

If we have not gone thoroughly through Step IV or have taken it too superficially, this can become a blockage both in getting to know our 'karmic being' better and when we embark on the practising phase. We then lack genuine motivation to act in a new way.

C. *Fearfulness*

New self-knowledge is always accompanied by uncertainty, anxiety or even fear, especially when it necessitates a new approach towards one's life. Anxiety then often appears when one is alone with oneself but this fear soon disappears if one looks it squarely in the face and busies oneself with an inner or outer activity.

D. Concentrating the will

Learning Step V calls for inner concentration in which we become aware of what and how we intended to practise. We can be blocked from doing what we intended either by directing our soul forces too strongly towards the world around us or by too strongly directing our attention inwards. There are some exercises that can help us overcome these problems. The ability to collect one's thoughts in a concentrated way involves being aware of what one is doing while one is doing it. This is helped by preparing well and evaluating objectively.

E. Strong habits, compulsive behaviour, addictions etc.

These areas entail many levels and variations that carry strong resistances towards, as well as escapes from, transforming one's karma. Most of them are untransformed old karma which takes on a substitute behaviour. The resistance to transforming one's karma is unusually strong. Addictions—from workaholism to drug addiction—belong in the field of therapy and must be tackled there. Here we are concerned only with normal learning blockages that get in the way of our destiny exercises. But we soon discover that our 'doubles', which consist of undigested old karma, can be very similar to addictions in themselves, only not so strong. Among these are all our fixed ideas and concepts, the many feelings that are always the same on similar occasions, and every instinctive action. Professional deformations are often also part of 'old destiny' established in our present life. They are widespread, and Destiny Learning makes us aware of them, so that we can do something about them. The related learning blockages arise because we have not had much experience with them and know of no practical ways of transforming them. Psychotherapy has many methods of bringing about changes in behaviour, but few that use the client's independently recognized karmic causes as a starting point. These are the ones that bring about healing, whereas a change of behaviour as such often only shifts the problem; the behaviour is changed, but the problem remains.

F. Karmic 'feeling-memory'

When we first meet someone, it often happens that a feeling arises in us either of great admiration and respect or of frustration and antipathy, or any nuance in between. Those involved in Destiny Learning should realize that feelings flaring up in this way have no external cause but are an inexplicable 'feeling-memory'. Unrecognized, such feelings constitute a learning blockage which can lead to unhappy or confusing social situations. Initial feelings of this kind are karmic memories related to past lives and not to our present life situation. As we practise we become more receptive to these 'feeling-memories'. But if we adapt our present behaviour to them, damning or glorifying someone as a result, this gives rise to a world of illusion that not only covers up today's reality but also prevents us from transforming the past in a way that is suitable for the present and thus also the future.

G. Changing our relationships

We have already remarked that our karmic exercises gradually make us aware of the destiny web in which we find ourselves. This can markedly affect our relationships with other people. Even in Step III the interpretation of cause and effect used by psychologists can become a serious learning blockage. This is because they relate sequences of cause and effect only to a person's present life and regard him or her as merely a product of the environment. Of course cause and effect are applicable to destiny, but only when they are seen to stem from former incarnations and from the post-mortem and pre-natal preparations leading up to and expressed in our present life.

Step V also requires us to practise our relationships with others. Then we become accustomed to this different understanding of karmic cause and effect and practise it daily. We stop working with concepts such as interaction, projection, repression, sublimation and other generalizing models of behaviour, for the powers of karma are intricately differentiated and vary from person to person. (It is worth noting that most of those models are borrowed from the laws of physics.)

As our web of destiny gradually becomes more visible to us, giving us at least an inkling of the karmic reality lying behind our relationships, many current psychological models turn out to be entirely inadequate to the task of understanding our human environment; they are more likely to cover up than reveal the complex forces of karma. Karma is the reality in which we live, and our normal understanding based on cause and effect is unable to form adequate concepts for it.

For many of us it is quite a shock to discover that we have been living in a world of imagined dreams and illusions with regard to our fellow human beings. We realize we have been living with people for years without understanding anything about their karmic reality, the reality of their destiny. Every individual bears within him a part of the other's destiny forces. How can we possibly appraise another human being correctly if we have recognized nothing about his or our own destiny?

There is a dense veil between people which we only gradually manage to lift after some time. The learning blockage consists in our unwillingness to drop the familiar models on which we base our intellectual interpretations and which have given us the false sense of certainty to which we have been accustomed for so long. We need to leave an 'open space' between perception and appraisal in which the karmic judgement can arise. In fact, allowing for an 'open space' is necessary for any kind of judgement to form, and it is recommended as a regular exercise in the adult learning process.

Arriving at judgements in connection with Destiny Learning is greatly complicated by the fact that when two individuals meet, the karma of each one comes into play, and in addition they may also be karmically linked in some way.

In such instances, the exercise involves overcoming the blockage brought into play by those models of interaction mentioned above. Then the realm of karmic forces can come into view.

H. Destiny as a sense-perceptible and a supersensible experience

We experience the powers of karma with increasing reality as we continue to practise the exercises. Having accepted their destiny in Step IV and voluntarily joined forces with it, many find that their present destiny appears to change. It worked differently prior to Step IV than it does once Step IV has been accomplished. Before Step IV the task was the focal point; thereafter destiny helps us more and becomes a guide on our path. This is because our 'karmic being' begins to give us indications. In consequence of this the weaving of karma appears as something quite extraordinary, namely a web of forces that are at once sense-perceptible and supersensible, heavenly and earthly, constantly alternating between matter and spirit.

Karma arises on the earth in consequence of our destructive or constructive actions; in the spiritual world it is then worked on with the help of all the powers of karma. Thereafter it reappears on the earth in order to be taken further by the education destiny affords us. This alternation is echoed in the day/night rhythm mentioned in connection with nighttime learning.

Those who are unable to regard the alternation of the threads of karma between a spiritual, supersensible world and a sense-perceptible, physical world as a reality will find it difficult to comprehend the reality of karma and how it works. Being unable to experience karma as a bridge between the two worlds then becomes a learning blockage. Positive affirmation of karma and its effects on future destiny can gradually remove this blockage, so that our learning through karma can become a guiding principle in our development.[9]

Learning Step VI

1. Growing ability to observe the karmic web
Through the regular, rhythmical practice of Step V combined with regular repetition of all the Learning Steps, new threads are constantly discovered, and these gradually fuse to form one single increasingly meaningful whole. A karmic web comes into view that has less and less to do with an isolated individual and more and more includes the destiny of one's fellow human beings.

In Learning Step VI our karmic horizon expands. Among the life processes the sixth was 'growing', and now in Destiny Learning our awareness of destiny grows; and with it grows our responsibility for transforming our past deeds into actions that will shape the future in a healing and harmonizing way. Those who have already trodden this path report how their awareness in the social realm grows through experiencing in a concrete way how very interlinked we all are in the web of destiny. In addition to experiencing this very real social dimension they also realize that unrecognized destiny chained to the past represents the greatest anti-social force. Undigested old karma is an obstacle not only for one's own development but also for the way one relates with other people. If Destiny Learning cannot become a lifelong learning process, the social future will indeed look bleak.

Eastern religions have always regarded karma merely as a balancing out of former failures. Once we see it as a process of learning and development on a human scale we discover that those very failings, even the worst, can serve to help us develop specific new faculties which could otherwise not arise. Karma is the great opportunity for us to develop ourselves. In Step III this was hinted at as a learning task; in Step V it was something to practise in everyday life. In Step VI, slowly but surely, the sense of destiny arises as the means with which one can steer future actions. We increasingly discover many different kinds of behaviour that are fruitful in this respect.

2. How does this new gift come to expression?
It shows itself in various ways. On the one hand many people are discovering the sense of destiny to be a kind of natural gift that appears suddenly without their having gone through any kind of learning process such as the one described in this book. You go somewhere and have a strong sense of having been there before; you meet someone and realize straight away that you have known him or her for a long, long time. These experiences of *déja-vu* are well-known, and they can be accompanied by the appearance of inner pictures showing past events, inexplicable fears in certain situations and so on. They can also arise while we are giving our detailed description of our chosen destiny event in Learning Step I. The path from Step I to Step IV serves, *inter alia*, to transform this natural gift into a learning process in which we can become fully conscious of destiny phenomena as they occur.

Some who have trodden the path described here have told how their sense of destiny first appeared when they were listening intently to another participant describing a destiny event, and that what mattered was not so much what was said as how it was said. You get a sense, an experience of karma forces showing through. At first you tend not to trust this observation, but after a while you learn to distinguish it from other perceptions because it has its own very specific quality. Little by little these impressions become a sense for destiny forces that you can trust just as much as your other senses. Initially it functions in isolated life situations and is triggered inspirationally by listening. Soon the impressions turn into visual images or even ideas and word pictures. As already mentioned several times, it is a good exercise if the person in question can confirm, correct or indeed refute these karmic impressions by putting forward many facts, experiences and phenomena.

3. How does the destiny sense develop?
Learning Step VI rests on a life process that is expressed by the concept 'growing'. In the learning process this equates with the possibility of consciously taking 'some-

thing' in and causing it to grow through exercises until it becomes a capability. Then that 'something' is not just any capability but the specific faculty of being able to observe karmic forces. It is possible to comprehend reincarnation and karma in the sense of a growth principle as a gift from spiritual powers who want to open up the path of development for us. Genuine human evolution is unthinkable without reincarnation and karma. Therefore considerable development in our daily functioning becomes possible when our sense for destiny lights up for the past and the future.

4. Activities to support the development of the destiny sense

a) The independent adult learning path is a necessary preparation for the learning path of self-knowledge described here in which selfless observation has special significance.

b) Aesthetic judgement forming can be an especially useful support for developing the sense of destiny. This is because we practise it in all kinds of different and changing situations. Judgement forming is then enhanced and refined until it becomes capable of observing destiny forces.

c) Any exercise that gives us experiences of metamorphosis both in nature and in the soul is especially important.

d) A thorough study of the laws of reincarnation and karma will show us how we can experience and perceive them in reality.

5. How to handle the destiny sense
Once we have learnt to hear and see destiny phenomena in our environment we begin to experience an entirely new world that is much more real for us than the one we have known up to now. How we handle it has consequences not only for ourselves but also for our fellow human beings. A new type of social behaviour is needed to fit our observations of destiny. We can no longer do without that 'open space' between observation and judgement which has been

mentioned several times already. The way we behave can either block a destiny situation entirely, making it chaotic and illusory, or it can clarify, help, redeem and heal such a situation. More and more possibilities for action open up, but choosing which one to apply gets increasingly difficult as our responsibility grows. It also becomes increasingly obvious how damaging it is to make pronouncements about karma when no process of adult learning has taken place in advance.

Responding impulsively or acting on the basis of some firm conviction, as we have been in the habit of doing, proves to be rather arbitrary and unsuitable in karmic situations. What we now need is a new, creative social ethic, for which Learning Step VII will offer a learning possibility.

Learning Step VII

1. Being creative in bringing order into destiny

The aim and result of the seven steps of Destiny Learning are intended to be: our ability to act freely and creatively in the destiny situations life presents us with. First we gain greater proficiency in understanding the karmic web of a destiny situation. This in itself changes our experience of that situation, so that a space opens up in which alternative ways of behaving become possible.

It becomes essential to ask *how* we should act with our destiny and create future destiny. Since every situation is karmically different we have to be creative in how we act. Although there are general laws, destiny is actually different every day. Handling our destiny should become a deed that is creative for the future. Every action will have to give a creative answer to the destiny situation bestowed on us by the powers of destiny.

Being able to read the situation correctly is a faculty that was developed in Step VI of Destiny Learning. Which action will be harmonizing, balancing, healing or fruitful for the future is at first still unknown in any creative deed. There are four sources for us to draw on:

2. Destiny actions that create order
The first source of help is the realization that in the process of evolution the functioning of karma and reincarnation have their purpose in that the human being shall be able to make mistakes (the 'Fall'), learn from these and thus gradually attain freedom of action out of this. The consequence of our arbitrary handling of destiny is that disorder enters into the order of the universe. To fulfil our destiny is to achieve the profoundly significant aim of bringing order back into our destiny so that it can contribute to and integrate with the divine world's ordering. For many individuals this would mean that their actions would begin to bring about balance, make good, and bring harmony into the universe.

3. Destiny actions as the source of a social art
The second source of help offers insight not only into the past but also into the future. Evolution can be seen as a path towards freedom. Undigested old karma always shows up as a shackle, an unfreedom, while working through karma brings liberation and openness, as well as new abilities, for the future. It is also very important for the future that we should discover karma to represent a web encompassing the whole of humanity, so that we are all karmically linked with one another. The actions we take in destiny situations always result in consequences for our fellow human beings, as we discovered in the exercises of Learning Step V. To act karmically has a social dimension, a function connected with humanity's development. Such actions are the source of a new social art, where 'art' refers to the way every situation demands to be dealt with in a specific manner that answers the real question. The author of this book is of the opinion that no meaningful social future can arise without Destiny Learning. One of our guiding principles could be phrased as follows: 'Let us act in a way that enables others to untie the knots of destiny that bind them to us; let us act not only correctly but fruitfully for the future; let us act in a way that serves the aims of evolution.'

4. Destiny actions as healing deeds

A third source is the knowledge that to bring order into destiny is to place it meaningfully in the cosmic order. In the sense of the new (Christian) awakening of the will we introduce something new into the cosmos because we are doing it of our own free will in using a conscious learning process.[10] Someone acting through knowledge heals by bringing order into his destiny.

This is the foundation of true healing. As Gerhard Kienle put it: 'Healing is not a matter of going beyond the natural order; it is a matter of placing-oneself-correctly-into-the-cosmic-order.'[11] Only if we do this do we discover that Destiny Learning is after all a process of healing for man and the world, and that every biography contains a God-given healing process of learning. To place-oneself-correctly-into-the-cosmic-order is the learning task; and destiny itself is the medicine for it.

5. Destiny actions as a new conscience

The fourth source is a new awareness that has to do with our conscience. It could also be termed a more penetrating vision, a new clairvoyant vision with regard to the future. The new capability that arises in Learning Step VI relates to the past and how it becomes visible in the present. One could call it a karmic review. The new clairvoyance looks at the consequences our actions will have for the future. We develop it whenever we wrestle in despair with karmic decisions in hopeless situations. The author has frequently found that people actually know very well what they should do but that this awareness is buried underneath their intellectual arguments and body-bound emotions. They do not want to hear the voice of conscience rising up from their subconscious and telling them to do what appears to be illogical or unbearable. Destiny Learning brings the voice of conscience, what we 'already know', up to the surface where we can act in accordance with it. Night-time learning is once again a great help in this respect because it is during the night that karmic reality speaks to us.

One good exercise in this connection is to imagine a number of possible decisions as vividly as possible and then feel one's way around them in order to sense intuitively what the consequences of each would be. Usually images arise showing 'what might happen if ...'. To be able to see the consequences of one's actions in pictures is a natural gift many people have even without having followed a path of learning such as that described in this book. Such pictures can often appear as threats, pangs of conscience, premonitions of mischief, or also as euphorias, promises of happiness, confirmations of one's elite station, and so on. So this natural gift needs to be schooled if it is to work truthfully and accurately. It can then become the ability to see forward clearly into the karmic future, just as the capability in Learning Step VI served to look back into the karmic past. The Karmic Review and the Karmic Preview thus become each other's complement.

Both these capabilities together now form the arena in which decisions can be taken creatively with regard to what destiny demands: to act in freedom and to serve humanity. The future depends on our deeds, and the seven-part learning process should be a path towards deeds that increasingly serve to shape the future.

In this light Destiny Learning offers us a key to a new kind of social behaviour—not necessarily the only key nor the only path, but simply the one this author has been able to discover. To regard this as the only path would be tantamount to slamming the door in the face of many other forms of Destiny Learning. It will have achieved its aim if it can act as the gateway to many other forms still to come. The Destiny Learning introduced in this book is an introduction to learning from destiny during life. It is a kind of learning that should accompany us during the whole of life, leading us to ever deeper layers of understanding our true being.[12]

3. Basic Attitude to Destiny

Destiny Learning is a path to be followed by independent adults. A number of aspects must be taken into account if we are to follow the Seven Learning Steps of Destiny Learning:

a) It will surely be agreed that a basically moral attitude will be needed.
b) Discipline in learning is necessary. Speculation and sensationalism should be guarded against.
c) It is essential to have a positive attitude, since karma can all too easily appear as a matter of good and bad, guilt and atonement, mistakes and rewards. Only a non-judgemental attitude can enable us to recognize the meaning of destiny events. Seemingly negative things can have a positive significance for the future, and vice versa.
d) Although it is human beings who create the web of destiny encompassing the whole of humanity, it is the divine powers of destiny who guide its course. They bring to bear a degree of moral wisdom that transcends by far the little human yardsticks according to which we normally form our judgements.
e) Our positive attitude is strengthened when we are permitted to gain an inkling of the higher meaning of destiny. Then the karmic web of humanity appears to us as a web of love, the purpose of which is to open the way for humanity to attain freedom.
f) There is no telling whether we are all capable of treading this path of Destiny Learning. Experience has shown up obstacles that arise on the path of the seven Learning Steps. If the blockages appear insurmountable, help will be needed, for example from an experienced facilitator. A second form of help is through individual conversations, from counselling up to psychotherapy, provided it follows the same seven steps, although in a more therapeutic form. A third method that has been tried out successfully

is that of art therapy. It is essential for the therapist to know when the learning process must make way for a therapeutic approach and when conversation is called for.

Our 'Summary and Conclusion' will give an overall picture of the Seven Learning Steps again in another way to show that together they can become a living organic process for a deeper understanding of the human being and his mission.

4. Summary and Conclusion

Destiny Learning means learning a new language

Those who have practised Destiny Learning have often confirmed that it has led them to a new language in that they began to hear, listen and speak in a new way. Therapists in particular have gained much that is fruitful for them in this respect. Contributions in the group, often a single sentence, suddenly attained decisive significance through the way they arose out of the depth of another's experience of destiny.

Regarding Step I (listening to the words of destiny): Something finds expression when accurate inner and outer observations of a destiny event are combined; thus a new language is born. Any language creates a link, a bridge between our inner life and the outside world around us—this is what we call communication. When communication arises between something that comes towards us from outside and the answers we bring towards it from within, the language of destiny comes into being. But we do not understand it as well as we do the language we use in everyday life.

It is destiny that speaks in the encounter between an individual and the surrounding world.

In Step I we learn our first words in the language of destiny. Powers of karma resound in the manner in which someone describes an event—they resound in the voice timbre, the sentence structure and even in the images that are used. If we learn to listen out for these things we begin to hear the first words of destiny's language.

Regarding Step II: Now we begin the search for the destiny words that belong to our own biography. Have we heard them before? When and how? They may sound different depending on our age and circumstances, just as with everyday language we can use the same word or parts of a word for many expressions. This, though, is as far as we can take the analogy between destiny language and everyday language, for destiny actually speaks here in biographical pictures.

The language of destiny has a lofty origin for it was created by the powers of karma, so we must listen to it with reverence. It can become the language of human beings only when they have learnt to handle the events of their destiny more or less consciously. When this has been achieved one becomes capable not only of hearing but also of understanding the language of destiny. We discover not only word-pictures but a whole language of pictures, and we begin to realize that what this language is saying pertains to ourselves and to the world.

Regarding Step III: The language of destiny is a picture-language we have shared in creating during the course of our life. When we ask why we speak 'like this' in our biography, so uniquely in the alternation between inner and outer worlds, the picture-language recedes into the background and the 'speaker' as such becomes visible.

We then enter into a dialogue with ourself—and this is the beginning of genuine self-knowledge. We might ask: 'How did my destiny language come into existence, why is it being spoken to me at this particular moment and in this particular fashion? What is the future task it is trying to show me?' We become aware of our own origins, the significance of the present time, and the aim of our own life. We are listening to the language of our own destiny.

Regarding Step IV: Divine spiritual beings have bestowed the gift of speech on human beings. Everything has been created by the primeval language—known as the Logos. In olden times 'the Word' possessed magical powers. Holy Words were used to heal the sick and conduct religious rites. The ordinary language of today is becoming increasingly meaningless and void of content, and is far from any genuine communication.

Experiencing the language of destiny in Step III enables one to have an existential encounter with one's Self. It is our own individual language, but it is disharmonious and a distortion of the primeval language. As we listen to it, the will grows in us to transform our destiny language into a language of genuine healing for our fellow human beings, for the earth and for the cosmos. To practise genuine communication is to learn the new language of destiny. At the same time we also begin to guess at the future possibilities, the moral-magical effects of destiny's language.

The legend of Parzival presages the future task of destiny language. The narrative with its wonderful biographical images centres around the crucial question Parzival is expected to ask. When he finally manages to utter the question a healing event takes place that would have been impossible had he not spoken. He accomplished his destiny task by speaking that sentence—when speaking became a deed. Parzival was able to do this deed by 'speaking the right words' once he had learnt how to see, read and understand his destiny. His question: 'What ails thee, uncle?' could thus be taken to mean: 'I take your destiny as well as my own upon myself.'

Our resolve to learn the language of destiny is the culmination of Step IV.

Regarding Step V: We now begin to practise the new language and in doing so we daily come up against hindrances to speaking it, including obstacles we ourselves create and which therefore prevent us from being heard correctly. There is a profound bond between being able to speak and being able to shape one's destiny. The way we speak expresses the whole of our karmic potential. When we practise destiny consciously in everyday life we meet with countless obstacles. Practising how to overcome these obstacles is what leads to new capabilities, which in Step V are especially connected with perceiving karmic connections and relationships.

More and more we realize that 'how' something is said is much more important than 'what'. By listening to the language someone else speaks, we experience—usually in pictures—what that person's karmic links are. However, we have to practise continually to gain the ability to speak the language of destiny. As we practise, others begin to speak to us in destiny words. Then genuine communication begins to come about.

Regarding Step VI: As we proceed with this step we notice that our night-time learning transforms what we have practised during the day into capabilities for everyday life. We also observe how several incarnations begin to be perceived by ourselves as well as with others. The language of destiny grows ever more varied. We 'hear' whether someone lived an earlier life in an ancient Chinese, Red Indian, Asian, African, Greek or Scandinavian culture, for this will have karmically influenced the way that person speaks today. The way someone speaks can have echoes which are reminiscent of things that seem quite strange today. We must learn to listen with ever greater subtlety to 'how' someone speaks. Being able to speak, or at least understand, several of today's languages is a help in this respect.

Slowly but surely our language becomes a destiny language that lives in reality, and this enables us to have more profound encounters with others. All the social, teaching and therapeutic professions that depend on communication will have to regard this learning path as an essential ingredient in their future training programmes. It will be essential for counselling therapy and psychotherapy.

Regarding Step VII: In this step we attain the ability to handle the language of destiny in a way that creates order, healing and harmony in the destiny of both speaker and listener. Our language becomes alive and creative, and can join in shaping the moral future of humanity. Moral language brings order into our destiny. Firstly we have acquired a new ability to hear and see the web of destiny. Secondly we can now speak to others about destiny events in a free and objective way that enables people to hear what we are saying. Destiny communication becomes possible.

Our being of feeling and will becomes audible in 'how' we speak. In this being lives the second, our 'karmic being', who is expressed chiefly in the vowels. The vowels form the stream of air. When we breathe karmically through words—which means when we speak the language of destiny—communication becomes creative. Christ brings to us the creative, healing Word, the new and inspiring way of speaking.

Having been bound by blood relationships since the 'fall', human beings now become beings who can 'beget' through the Word.

Summary:

I read the Word
Step 1. I see a karmic Word (the gesture).
Step 2. I read this word in my biography.
Step 3. Only now do I comprehend this Word.
Step 4. It is my Word, and I want to learn how to speak it.

I speak the language
Step 5. I learn to speak my Word.
Step 6. I hear the language of destiny.
Step 7. I speak the language of destiny.

This new language came to expression in a verse Rudolf Steiner sent on his sixty-third birthday to his close friend and co-worker Ita Wegman.[13] We quote it here in conclusion:

Hearts will sense the meaning of karma	*Es deuten die Herzen das Karma*
When hearts learn	*Wenn die Herzen lernen*
To read the word	*Lesen das Wort*
Which shapes	*Das in Menschenleben*
Human life	*Gestaltet*
When hearts learn	*Wenn die Herzen reden*
To speak the word	*Lernen das Wort*
Which develops	*Das im Menschenwesen*
The human being.	*Gestaltet.*

One question that can be answered through spiritual research remains unanswered here. Why is the capability of this moral language of destiny present in seed form in our seven life processes? What we have shown in this book so far is how these forces can be brought to the surface through a learning process.[14]

Summary and Conclusion   135

Note One:
1. The author has described the importance of destiny work for our development as human beings in many lectures that can underpin the learning process. Some of the themes have been: The healing power of destiny work; Karma work as a path to self-knowledge; Destiny work as a source of social development for the future; Destiny learning as the heart of adult learning; etc.

2. There is a specific exercise that makes visible in words, speech and images our self-discovered past, our self-chosen future and the metamorphosis that takes place between the two. (See Part Four 'Some Exercises for Adult Learning and Destiny Learning'.)

3. Carefully chosen painting, modelling and eurythmy exercises can help make the process of acceptance a profound experience.

4. Many participants in seminars on 'Learning from Destiny' have experienced their work together as encouraging and strengthening.

Note Two:
Participants who have got to know the beginnings of Destiny Learning in their first seminar frequently now put in requests for follow-on seminars. Here they can exchange views with other participants about experiences they have had with all seven Learning Steps. This enables them to check, deepen and improve their own procedures. Methods have been developed to cater for this need, but they will not be discussed here. The need for such seminars is pressing because one's first seminar on 'Learning from Destiny' can really only be the initial step needed to learn the method.

Note Three:
Hitherto, adult educators who accompany and look after participants in Destiny Learning seminars have learned mainly 'on the job'. Plans are afoot to offer a properly structured course for this in the near future. The hope is that

soon the path of Destiny Learning will be incorporated into all adult education in some form, and then many facilitators will be needed.

Note Four:

The relationship of Destiny Learning with the seven professional fields of the adult educator described in Part One
The adult educator's seven professional fields play an important part in Destiny Learning. Some aspects are summarized here.

a) Step I of Destiny Learning calls for accurate inner and outer observation if the learning process is to proceed properly (Professional Field I). Observation is what counts, not the intrusion of subsequent memories and interpretations. Even at this stage self-knowledge becomes an enhancement of ordinary knowledge and the normal learning process; this increases in subsequent steps. Observation of the 'gesture' must have a quality that can achieve a synthesis.

b) Step II requires a further enhancement of observation (Professional Field I) so that relevant symptoms can be related to the passage of time.

c) Step III calls for a judgement forming capacity that extends aesthetic judgement forming to include empathy, and even beyond (which represents a deepening of Professional Field II).

d) In Step IV the ability to encounter others is enhanced further to include self-encounter (Professional Field III). Facilitators have repeatedly insisted that in accompanying the individualization process both the sense of truth and competence in the other two learning paths (Vocational Learning and Spiritual Research Learning, i.e. Professional Field IV) are essential. Accepting destiny requires one to adopt an attitude of research with regard to one's own destiny.

e) As mentioned above, Step V calls for the work to be deepened through night-time learning (Professional Field

Summary and Conclusion 137

VI). One must be fairly familiar with night-time learning in order to use it correctly in Step V. The same applies to Step VI.

f) In Destiny Learning, Step VII is the crown and aim of the other six steps. One must now be able to combine the two sides of reality, of day-time and night-time learning, in order to proceed creatively.

g) One can envision:
—Steps I, II and III as the path of discovery towards the powers of destiny;
—Steps III, IV and V as the way to practise self-knowledge;
—Steps V, VI and VII as a path of development towards freedom.

The adult educator's seven professional fields thus play an important part in Destiny Learning as a path to self-knowledge.

Part Three:
The Adult Educator's Schooling Path

1. The Threefold Relationship Between Adult Educator and Participants

We have mentioned a number of times that the type of adult education under discussion here urgently needs adult educators who have been schooled properly in this new profession. Every profession calls for expert knowledge and skills as well as personal qualities and capabilities that have to be developed. Every profession also has its own moral ethos. Professional ethics in other professions are dwindling and only remnants remain, for example in the medical and teaching professions. Yet they are still as important as ever, so for a new profession like that of the adult educator they should be conceptualized afresh. In the following we shall endeavour to formulate this as well as ideas about schooling the new adult educator him or herself.

1.1 Relating to one's own profession

Adult educators must realize that when they move from their present profession to that of teaching adults their basic attitude will have to undergo a change. They will now be aiming for a different goal. Hitherto their specialism will have been their main concern, but now it is those they are going to work with who must occupy centre stage. Their specialism remains important but is nevertheless now secondary, being a means of serving the development of fellow human beings. The changeover can bring about inner conflict, for entering the profession of educator entails relinquishing things that are very dear to one. The dilemma becomes all the more obvious when we take into account that loving our special subject is essential if we are to teach it to someone else. Nevertheless, the adult educator's main aim now is to help other human beings attain professional, psychological and spiritual development.

The more we school ourselves to allow not only specialist knowledge but also Destiny Learning and Spiritual Research Learning to flow into our profession of adult educator, the more we realize the need to transform the basic attitude of teaching a specialist subject into one that serves the development of other individuals. Even if we continue to work in our old profession, as many do, we cannot avoid undergoing this change of attitude.

This does not mean to say that the adult educator's own specialism becomes any less important. On the contrary: the very fact that we suffuse our vocational teaching with what the other two learning paths can bring will make our present and future profession immensely deeper and richer.

1.2 Creating a threefold relationship between adult educator and adult participant

Adult learning must allow a new relationship between adult educator and adult learner to arise. Let us call the adult learner a 'participant' since he participates in a learning process as a self-responsible individual.

The relationship between teachers and students at many universities and technical colleges—in fact in most teaching situations—has been problematical for many years. Student protests and unrest involving violence on both sides are a sign of the times. They show that deep and often instinctive forces are at work in the relationship between adult educators and participants. These forces stem from the past and are now acting as obstacles to a new and more contemporary form of relationship.

I shall point out in the following that these obstacles and problems exist on both sides—students and teachers—and often mutually exacerbate one another.

For a better understanding let us look at the roles played by pupils and teachers in former cultures. In ancient times the teacher was someone who brought divine wisdom to the people. The wisdom came from above; it was a religious revelation, so the one who passed it on came to be regarded

The Threefold Relationship 143

and revered as a more highly developed person. The further back we go in time, the more does this basic attitude come to the fore. Ancient tradition even has it that the gods themselves originally taught us everything. Where now we have professors, lecturers, teachers, educators or trainers there were formerly priests, pharaohs, the initiate, the guru, the mandarin and so on. They were the bearers of lofty wisdom and possessed absolute authority. Meanwhile the recipients of the wisdom, the adepts, chelas, apprentices or students, absorbed the higher revelations with great reverence and devotion. Doubts, criticism, independent work or verification were regarded as inadmissible. Independent individual learning like that expected nowadays was not yet on the agenda.

It is not hard to see that these two attitudes of bygone times live on in people, often unconsciously and instinctively. Which of us does not want to be shown the right way by someone who knows? Which of us would not rather like to point out the correct path to someone else? Having discovered through Destiny Learning how strongly that old teacher/pupil relationship lives on in us from former incarnations, we need not be surprised at the blockages that now stand in the way of a contemporary relationship between adult educator and adult participant. Therefore both must cultivate a basic attitude that can overcome step by step their karmic bonds with former cultures.

We shall now look more closely at how the three learning paths each demand a different relationship between adult educator and participant.

The relationship in Vocational Learning
We can begin with the adult educator in Vocational Learning.

In earlier days this was the person who passed on knowledge and skills to others. Today he must become the one who enables other adult human beings to follow their independent path of learning. To awaken and facilitate their path of learning he must be skilled in offering them practical aids that can act as the catalyst for the adult learning process.

What the adult educator has to offer is a means and no longer an absolute content. The facts he passes to the participants, for example, are not intended to be stored exactly as given and then reproduced in identical form at a later date. Their purpose is to enable development processes to take place in the participants themselves, processes over which the adult educator has no control, nor should he have. The adult educator thus increasingly becomes an instrument for the participants to use in their own independent way. The adult educator has to climb down from his high horse! His task is to encourage independent learning and to become an instrument for this. It is all the easier to climb down from that high horse when one realizes what an important task it is to enable another human being to attain freedom in his or her own learning process. This even applies in the realm of Vocational Learning. To become a good instrument for the participants, an adult educator must re-cast his knowledge and skills into suitable tools for the purpose.

As mentioned earlier, participants for their part also experience considerable inhibitions in developing a new learning attitude. It is quite off-putting, and indeed frightening, to be called upon all the time to make one's own decisions, take risks and be responsible for one's own learning process. So participants in their turn have great reservations about independent learning. In former incarnations the pupil was someone who received what was to be learnt gratefully, as a revelation. But now participants must awaken in themselves a free spirit of investigation and research, encouraged by the adult educator. The author knows only too well how strongly some participants almost force one to continue plodding along the old path, giving answers instead of awakening questions, prescribing methods instead of showing new paths that must be trodden independently, working in ways that invite imitation instead of encouraging a kind of learning that leads to individual development.

Evidently schooling ourselves is something best practised together with others. Adult educator and participants must agree with one another as to how they will proceed, for one cannot offer teaching that challenges people to be free in their work if those people do not want any freedom.

Conversely, it is very difficult for participants to be independent in their learning if the adult educator does not work in that direction. So it is up to the participants constantly to practise taking on full responsibility for their own learning process. The adult educator, for his part, must create possibilities and become a useful instrument which the participants become capable of using, as shown in Diagram 7.

Adult educator

Becoming an instrument

Able to be an instrument

Being an enabler

Vocational Learning
Putting the relationship on to a professional footing.

Participants

Being responsible for one's own learning process

Willing to be responsible

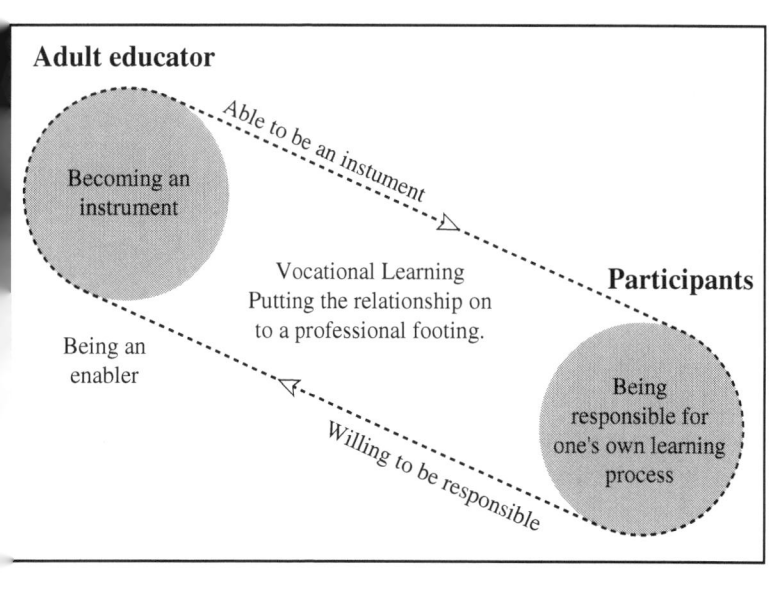

Diagram 7

1. The adult educator is shown in the top part of the drawing because he brings with him something that the participants need and want to acquire. This is the only sense in which 'higher' and 'lower' determine the relationship, since the learning process in itself increasingly functions horizontally.
2. The participants must learn to hold conversations that transcend any feelings of sympathy or antipathy. To

optimize the learning process it is essential to discuss how the adult educator can give of his best and how the participants can best learn. The way conversations are conducted puts the relationship on to a professional footing.

The relationship in Destiny Learning

Structuring the relationship between adult educator and participants in Destiny Learning is another matter. In Part Two of this book quite a bit has been said about accompanying group processes, but in the present section we shall be concerned primarily with how to handle the mutual destiny shared by adult educator and participants.

If we want our learning process to result in a genuine transformation, this means in practice that our soul life will have to go through a number of crises and changes during the learning processes; indeed, these crises are often actually caused by the schooling. The more effective it is, the more will it lead to profound transformations of one's inner world. It is therefore not on for the adult educator to maintain—as many do—that these crises are a personal matter for the participants, for which the adult educator bears no responsibility. It is the adult educator who has shared in bringing these crises about, so he should regard them as an integral part of the adult education. The participants are not only participants in a course but also fellow human. For the participants, on the other hand, the adult educator is not only an instrument used for the purpose of waking them up but also a fellow human being. In this sense the way destiny weaves between both parties is an essential element in adult education, if not actually the main component.

In the first place the relationship between the two must be consciously cultivated, as must all human relationships. So work must be done on any misunderstandings, irritations and frustrations as well as on the blockages deriving from the historical causes discussed earlier, and for this work to be possible there must be an objective relationship of equality. In this sense what was an exclusively pro-

The Threefold Relationship 147

fessional relationship must now be put on to a personal footing. We are not talking about the learning process but about the mutual relationship. The adult educator endeavours to become a 'fellow human being' of the participants. He will have to practise this, which assumes that he has a degree of psychological maturity. There are many inhibitions that obstruct this and it is very tempting to hide behind the role of 'teacher'.

The participants, equally, have a good deal to overcome before they are able to accept their adult educator as a human being with plenty of strengths and weaknesses. Both blinkered admiration and cynical condemnation are well-known enemies of a healthy and realistic relationship. One way of bringing about this healthy relationship is the 'helping conversation', which is not psychotherapeutic sessions but a conversation between equals. Adult educators need to learn how to conduct these helping conversations, and some educational establishments actually use such conversations as part of their programme. Similar elements are already established in various forms of 'tutorial' teaching, at least to the degree that students are given someone whom they can approach when necessary.

These helping conversations are only a part of the solution, however. To take account of the full reality of human relationships we must consciously include the powers of karma. In this sense being someone's friend and fellow human takes on a deeper dimension. The adult educator has to recognize the reality of the participant's destiny, the participant that of the adult educator, and both together the destiny they have in common through the learning process they find themselves in. Out of this arise questions regarding past karma and the shaping of present and future karma. It is a relationship in which the two are equal as they work together, and they will probably notice how much of any learning is in fact Destiny Learning. Diagram 8 (over) shows this pictorially.

1. The adult educator must be schooled to be familiar with 'karma forces' so that he can understand them when they

```
┌─────────────────────────────────────────────────────────┐
│  Adult educator      Able to handle      Participants   │
│        ╭╌╌╌╌╌╌╌╌╌╌╌╌╌  destiny  ╌╌╌╌╌▷╌╌╌╌╌╌╌╮         │
│       ╱ Willing to                    Willing to ╲      │
│      │ become a fellow  Destiny Learning  work at │     │
│      │ human being    Putting the relationship  achieving │
│       ╲              to a human footing  self-knowledge ╱│
│        ╰╌╌╌╌╌╌╌╌╌◁╌╌ Willing to encounter and ╌╌╌╌╌╯   │
│  Being a friend       accept as a fellow human being    │
└─────────────────────────────────────────────────────────┘
```

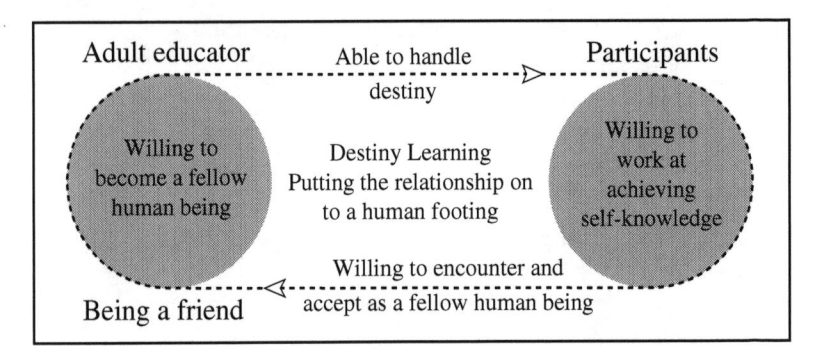

Diagram 8

come into play during the mutual learning process as well as treat them adequately as a form of self-knowledge.

2. The participants, on the other hand, must be willing to tread the path of Destiny Learning which will bring with it a considerable enhancement of their self-knowledge. Self-knowledge is a part of adult learning. In practice it has been found that the blockages here are not as intractable as they are in Vocational Learning so long as the human relationships are properly taken care of.

The relationship in Spiritual Research Learning
The relationship between adult educator and participants is different again in Spiritual Research Learning. The starting point is the adult educator's discovery that almost all the participants have had spiritual experiences in one form or another. One third of them will have had these experiences fairly consciously, another third will have been partially aware of them, and the final third will have them in a slumbering state. As time goes on this situation in which there is an interplay of sense-perceptible and super-sensible experiences will occur with increasing frequency. To include Spiritual Research Learning involves giving conscious answers about these tendencies that are beginning to awaken in people quite naturally.

How does the path of Spiritual Research Learning influence the relationship between adult educator and participants and how can this relationship be shaped in a healthy way?

One initial step is surely to give proper and factual information about those supersensible experiences. What types of experience are there? How do they come about? How do they influence our learning blockages? How can we observe and understand it when we 'step across the threshold'? And so on.

Obviously the adult educator must develop himself very thoroughly in order to become knowledgeable and experienced in matters of the threshold. The author has found that many adult educators are insufficiently prepared in this field even though these experiences are of a kind that can occur in any type of adult education. In fact the learning itself frequently triggers such experiences. There would be no need to hold seminars on 'How to deal with supersensible experiences' if such things were included in every programme.

One's basic attitude towards such experiences is just as important as giving factual information about them. There has to be a learning, searching basic attitude just like that described in connection with Vocational Learning and Destiny Learning. The Seven Steps of the adult learning process can also be applied to supersensible experiences, but this is not something the adult educator should preach about; he should work towards helping the participants experience this themselves. He must help them feel inspired about such experiences, but this calls for a new type of relationship.

Spiritual experiences are connected with the spiritual path along which someone is progressing. Every spiritual path has its own colouring. It is entirely individual, but there is a great danger of the adult educator imposing his own path on to the participants and of the participants setting the adult educator up as their leader. This is another example of why it is so important for Vocational Learning and Destiny Learning to take the form of a preparation for maintaining one's independence in Spiritual Research Learning as well.

The adult educator has to be a servant, a helping adviser along the other's path. He is subservient to that path, thus learning that the other's path is unique. The aim of this relationship is gradually to establish an attitude of colleagueship.

So the adult educator follows a threefold schooling path: from being an enabler to being a friend, and then to being a servant. He must be able to take on the roles of being an instrument, a fellow human being, and a research colleague. The author is quite aware of how much he owes to many participants for what he learned from them on his own schooling path and of the important contribution their supersensible experiences have made to his spiritual research. While being participants they were also colleagues whether they realized it or not. The relationship between adult educator and participants becomes ever more balanced and equal. This mutual give and take, this giving and receiving of advice, this exchange of research results and experiences will eventually be the foundation on which any relationship amongst colleagues is based. The participants learn from this what it is like to be an active member of a research group. In spiritual research especially one is dependent on collaboration amongst colleagues. This is a subject that will be worked out in more detail in the author's next book.

Experience has shown how damaging to the soul those confusing, illusory and destructive supersensible experiences can be if one has not learnt how to work with them through spiritual research. The basic attitude of spiritual research offers protection that can generate courage, self-confidence and inner certainty. But most people do not automatically possess this basic attitude. It has to be learnt, and it is the task of Spiritual Research Learning to bring this about. Participants must learn to become independent research colleagues and to understand that this entails one of the main faculties of their spiritual independence. Thus, even in the way the relationship between adult educator and participants is formed, this third learning path can become a force capable of coping with the many confusing inner and outer events of our present time. Diagram 9 shows this in the form of a picture:

```
                    Able to be a colleague in spiritual research
                                                                    Participants
    Adult              Spiritual
  educator       Research Learning
              Putting the relationship on
                  to a spiritual footing
                    Willing to be a colleague in spiritual research
Being a servant
```

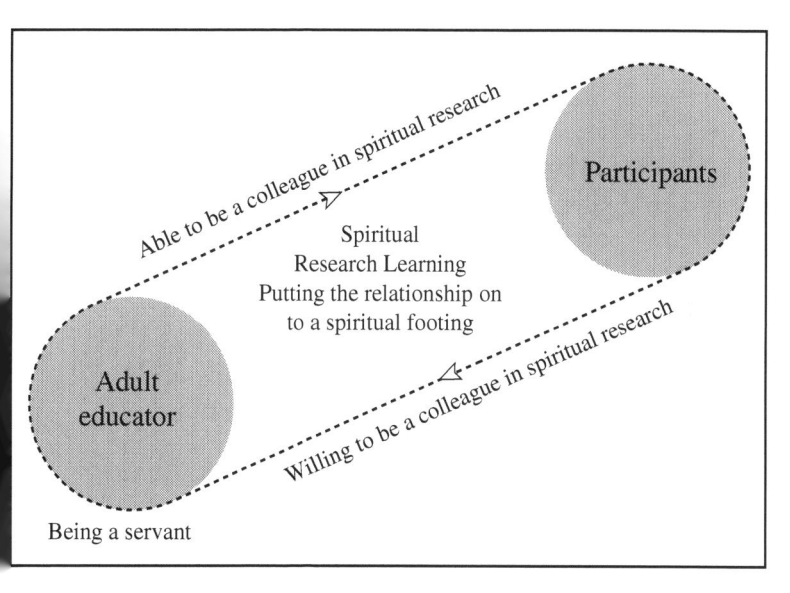

Diagram 9

1. The adult educator's schooling requires him to have a basic attitude of spiritual research, which is actually the jewel in the crown of adult learning. He must also develop himself to be proficient in threshold experiences. This is achieved through 'threshold psychology', also called 'spiritual psychology', which is a branch of psychology that is developing fast. The development that takes place during night-time learning is also very important here.
2. The adult participants must be willing to give expression to intimate spiritual experiences in a form in which they can be used as spiritual learning and research material. This is something many people do not find it easy to do. Assistance can be given through, for example, helping conversations, art therapy or other means.

Summary

To help the reader gain an overview, Diagram 10 shows the three types of relationship between adult educator and participants in a single picture through which they can be experienced as a totality.

The first relationship promotes independence and self-responsibility. The second nourishes and cultivates on-going self-knowledge. The third is intended as encouragement towards creative activity for the future. The three relationships build on one another. Each subsequent stage is an enhancement of the previous one. Both the adult educator and the participants must learn not to mix the three relationships since each one serves different aims. Much flexibility is therefore required.

Diagram 10 gives an inkling of what the professional profile or guiding image of the adult educator might become in the future. Frequent meditation on this image and its appli-

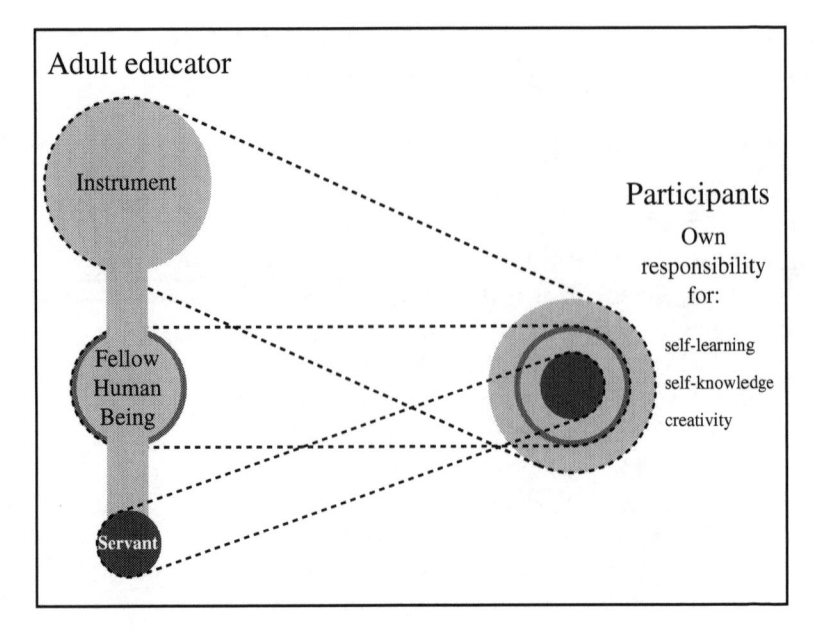

Diagram 10

cation in practice can contribute greatly to the adult educator's schooling path.

A schooling for adult educators might begin with the theme 'Learning how to learn'. Within this it would be very important to ask: 'How can we, with each other as well as with our future participants, shape our threefold relationship?' This would be especially helpful in conjunction with some initial simple exercises which can be deepened later on.

Initial experiences have shown that this could provide the basis for an entirely new adult education culture on which much could be built up.

2. Four Kinds of Time: Rhythm in Adult Education[1]

One of the most healthy influences we can have on daily life is to form our time consciously in a rhythmical way, whereas the least healthy life-style is one in which *time* determines *us* through experiences such as 'pressure of time', having 'no time', or by tyrannizing us to keep to spans of time we have determined in advance. The consequence of these is stress, panic, nervousness etc. Since adult educators usually have to work within prescribed timeframes, the ability to structure time rhythmically is an important ability to be learnt. They must also be able to help their course participants learn to do this because time is becoming increasingly difficult to handle in our technological culture. Dealing with time is a prophylactic measure that must be included in courses with adults.

In examining our relationship to time we discover that there are four different kinds of time. Being able to understand these and distinguish between them provides a fruitful entry into transforming time *pressure* into dealing with our time *rhythmically*.

2.1 Clock time

By using clocks we relate to time as a measurable commodity, dividing it up into seconds, minutes, hours, days, weeks, months, years and so on. Time is regarded as quantitative and thus controllable. We imagine that dividing and subdividing it gives us a firm grip on it. A timetable for teaching is a good example: 'I have x number of hours in which I can give out x amount of subject matter.'

Unfortunately, however, clock time is unreal. We have invented it as a straight-jacket by which to keep real time under control. No ancient culture ever lived under time constraints to match those we have created for ourselves today. Clock time constitutes a violation of real time. We have imprisoned ourselves in clock time and made it into a cultural disease. No clock can accurately replicate time, for in reality nature always brings in slight variations. The planetary orbits, for example, are never absolutely determined by clock time but are always subject to very slight shifts.

2.2 Living time or rhythm

We get closer to the true nature of time by regarding it as something qualitative. This second way of looking at time sees it as rhythm, as nature's time, or living time. Rhythm is a repetitive cycle, an alternation of increase and decrease, and every rhythm is embedded in other rhythms that influence and vary it. The real time in which we live is that of unspoilt nature, and in so far as we are living beings we are a part of this. The bearer of time processes in nature is the etheric realm, and in the human being it is the etheric body. If only we could follow the rhythms of the etheric body we should be able to live in an entirely healthy way. Unfortunately, however, we are also under the influence of other manifestations of time which make it less easy for us to live naturally and rhythmically within it.

2.3 Psychological time

The way we experience time is termed 'psychological time'. A boring conversation 'lasts forever', while a lively, interesting one 'makes time fly'. Our feelings constantly influence our natural 'living time'. Joy, sorrow and other emotions put their stamp on how we experience time, for example when we have to wait or are obliged to hurry. A manager once chided a younger employee who came to work late by suggesting that he might take an older colleague who had never been late in 40 years as a role model. The younger man almost lost his job when he suggested that the older colleague must have been suffering from a compulsive disorder.

Our psychological awareness seems to be a destructive

element where living, natural time rhythms are concerned because it makes us experience time as something which it is not. Anxiety, tension and nervousness are tiring, destructive forces. Since stress leads to exhaustion, psychological time must be regarded as an opponent of living time. But what is actually happening? The problem arises when psychological time latches on to clock time, creating a short-circuit. The living time between the two is destroyed, and this leads to breakdown, tiredness and exhaustion. Our insatiable urge to tie down the future by means of fixed plans, and our endless worry and tension when these plans do not work out (which is nearly always) point to a malaise in our civilization that will have to be overcome. Luckily there is a fourth kind of time that can come to our assistance.

2.4 Ego time

The fact that we can observe, experience and study time as a phenomenon shows that a part of our being lives in a situation which makes it independent of both time and space. Our ego is able to comprehend concepts such as time, space, eternity, duration and so on because it is independent of all these. Therefore our ego not only feels (figure III in Diagram 11) and understands time, but can also structure it.

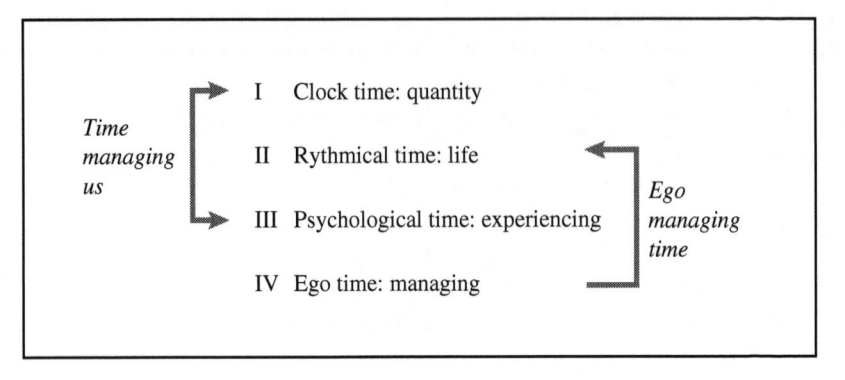

```
                    I    Clock time: quantity
    Time
    managing        II   Rythmical time: life
    us                                                  Ego
                                                        managing
                    III  Psychological time: experiencing   time

                    IV   Ego time: managing
```

Diagram 11

Four Kinds of Time: Rhythm in Adult Education

This brings us to our immediate concern, which is to find out how an adult human being can learn to handle the processes of living time in a healthy way.

We began this chapter with two statements: 'One of the most healthy influences we can have on daily life is to structure our time consciously in a rhythmical way,' and 'The least healthy life-style is one in which *time* structures *us.*' So now the question is: How can we use our ego to structure time? Diagram 11 relates to this.

In what way can adult educators school themselves in managing time, and how can they pass on to others what they themselves have learnt? Every learning situation should involve at least some preliminary work on this.

To bring about a connection with ego time we can practise exercises that lead to inner quiet and inner balance, and also strengthen our ability to concentrate. There are also meditations that strengthen our ego. One important consequence of these exercises can be the ability of our inner being to step outside time or rise above it.

It is also necessary for our ego to establish a new relationship with living time, and one good way of doing this is to study in detail the rhythms of nature and also soul processes that are rhythmical.[2] By doing this we become aware of living, natural time, which can be as though switched off or blocked when there is a short circuit between clock time and psychological time. With the help of natural time the ego can structure time.

A third element is the structuring of time in learning and working practice. Here is a simple example. Six young women in a spinning mill had to work together at a machine that ran at the same speed all day long (clock time). The setting conformed to a normed average. One day the women asked to be allowed to set the speed themselves because they preferred to vary their speed of work. They promised that their output would remain the same. The foreman agreed to break with tradition and try the experiment. The results were astonishing:

a) The women were quite capable of setting the speed of the machine to suit their own changing rhythm, and took their own short rest breaks when it suited them.
b) They were considerably less tired by the end of the day.
c) They enjoyed their work more (and the morale of the group improved).
d) To the foreman's amazement productivity rose considerably beyond the measured norm.

Applying this to a seminar situation, an adult educator might try to bring rhythm into each of the learning elements. A rhythmical process provides a living foundation for a seminar.

All the lectures, exercises, group sessions and conversations, all the artistic activities and the beginning and ending of each day must be governed by rhythms and related rhythmically with one another. One way of doing this is to work with repetition, but not rigidly, for repeating cycles are never identical since they are always influenced by other rhythms. Rhythms also involve increasing and decreasing speeds. There are changeover points, rest periods (open spaces) in which acceleration turns into deceleration and vice versa. This is very useful for structuring lessons. For the rest it has to be said that the rhythmical structuring of time remains a wide-open and very varied field waiting to be researched.

Another area relevant to the structuring of ego time is that of the seven Professional Fields discussed in Part One. Although it is exceedingly important, the structuring of time was not included as an eighth professional field since it has to imbue all the fields. This is obvious from the very way each of these builds on the next. Right at the beginning, perceiving is in itself a matter of rhythm. And a rhythmical process is similarly needed to create an open space between perceiving and forming a judgement.

An encounter between human beings is also a rhythmical process. Entirely new rhythms should arise through the ever-changing ways in which the three learning paths connect and disconnect. And finally day-time and night-time learning is in

Four Kinds of Time: Rhythm in Adult Education 159

itself a primeval ego rhythm which, though, we have to bring about ourselves by means of our learning activity.

Perhaps these suggestions can help support the adult educator's rhythmical schooling path. His aim is to help every adult participant learn to structure the rhythms of life independently through his ego. The consequences both for our culture and for our own individual health would be immeasurable.

3. Self-Education of the Adult Educator

Most adult educators will need to design their own development plan simply because there is as yet no regular course for them. One way of proceeding would be to take Professional Field VII 'Ability to shape the sevenfold learning process' and use this to work through Professional Fields I to VI. In other words: make each of these fields into a learning aim to be taken through the seven learning processes. There are a number of advantages to proceeding in this manner:

1. You are able to design your own learning plan and discover any gaps as you go along.
2. You try out on yourself what you want to teach future participants and discover, often with the help of colleagues, how to overcome your own learning blockages. The more thoroughly you do this the more will you be able to become an instrument for others.
3. By doing this you individualize these fields (Learning Step IV) and can then use them creatively (Learning Step VII) in your work, but only if you go through the seven learning processes sufficiently thoroughly.
4. This comprehensive self-education could also serve as a model for adult educators in which the whole learning process might be realized in concrete modules.

Examples and suggestions

Here is an example of how to work with the first Professional Field called 'Selflessly using the twelve senses':

1. I observe the range of all 12 senses known to me and available for my use, making myself aware of the ones in which I have not had much practice.
2. I ask myself which of the 12 senses I feel more at ease with and which are less familiar. This is best done by taking

Self-Education of the Adult Educator 161

examples from my life that illustrate this and can be used in the next step.
3. I endeavour to understand my talents and the gaps in my ability from the point of view of destiny. What did I bring with me, what is underdeveloped and what is entirely absent? What are the karmic causes for this?
4. I accept the result and agree that in one respect or another I have an urgent learning task as a candidate adult educator; this gives me the necessary motivation to practise.
5. With the help of colleagues and experts I look for suitable exercises; I design a concrete plan that will include attendance at suitable courses or seminars.
6. I regularly check the level at which my powers of observation are ready for use in adult education work—whether Vocational Learning, Destiny Learning or Spiritual Research Learning. Where necessary my learning plan can be adapted accordingly.
7. I evaluate where and when I am already capable of creatively furthering the participants' powers of perception. I note the situations in which I am not yet ready to do this.

We experience something important here, which is that the greatest rewards result from work on our greatest hindrances, gaps or incapacities. In addition, hitherto dormant capacities are often suddenly activated. As we become creative in one area, this has a favourable effect on other areas as well.

*

Let us now turn to an example of how to work with the second Professional Field, 'Independently developing the three judgement processes':

1. a) I ascertain which of the three judgement processes is most familiar to me and which I am not so good at.
b) I also ascertain how many methods and means are available to me so that I can use my 'independence' in this area in a way that helps others develop it too.
This form of self-evaluation can be used regularly in all

seven Professional Fields, so I can use it to check what level I have reached as an adult educator. I must observe this accurately and form a correct and honest assessment.
2. Judgements emanate from the middle part of the human being, in the life of feeling. So schooling the life of feeling as an organ of balance for judgement forming is the task of the adult educator that must be emphasized in this field. I assess my psychological aptitude in this respect.
3. Initially various unconscious convictions, values and prejudices brought with me from previous incarnations prevent me from forming independent judgements. Prolonged, thorough Destiny Learning is essential so that I can extricate myself from karmic determinations. Specific learning exercises need to be developed to help us become aware of our unconscious convictions and their origins.
4. In learning to be an adult educator I must also become aware of and accept my own one-sided traits in this field.
5. If I can overcome the spiritual determinism I carry karmically within me I shall be able to show the participants how to arrive at independent judgements that are free from karmic one-sidedness. (See the article by L. Bos in Part Four.)
6. My new capacities for forming judgements first become obvious in Vocational Learning as such, thereafter in the self-knowledge of Destiny Learning, and finally in Spiritual Research Learning, where inner objectivity of judgement is most urgently required. I endeavour to ascertain which level of teaching practice I have reached.
7. These endeavours come to fruition in the ability to work creatively in shaping varying processes in teaching practice. The author can confirm from experience that the three forms of judgement forming will manifest quite differently in the work of the adult educator in Africa, China, America or Europe. Nevertheless, in our age the sources and underlying principles are the same everywhere, for their characteristics stem from the human being as such.

*
As regards the adult educator's work in Professional Field III we can refer the reader to S. Routledge's article in Part Four which describes the seven ego-activities that must be schooled if we are to achieve the ability to encounter other human beings. Much still awaits development in this area. Specific exercises and methods need to be found through which the seven ego-activities can be developed. Here once again the seven learning processes described in the previous two examples can be used as a basis.

*

A description of the schooling and teaching needed for an integration of the three learning paths (Professional Field IV) will have to wait until the next book, on Spiritual Research Learning, in which this integration will be worked out in more detail.

*

We now come to an example of how to combine day-time and night-time learning (Professional Fields V and VI):

Here the adult educator has to build a bridge between the seven Learning Steps and day-time and night-time learning. The first step is to carry out a review at the end of the day in which the questions to ask are:

I. What have I learnt today?
II. How did I learn it?
III. What new question arises in me as a result?

It is a good idea to write down the answers so as not to forget them.

At the beginning of the next day one then considers what change these have undergone during night-time learning. Night-time learning can deepen yesterday's learning process, correct it or bring up new thoughts, answers and questions.

Experience has shown that these two exercises, repeated daily, can lead to an astonishing deepening and acceleration of the adult learning process. This is further intensified by endeavouring to understand how the seven learning processes continue during the night, undisturbed by day-time consciousness. After we fall asleep a backward review of the day takes place in our etheric body, and this continues until we wake up again.[3] When we have carried out the seven life/learning processes during the day through the exertions of our ego, it stands to reason that these learning processes are strengthened and completed during the night. The difficulty lies in how to harvest the fruits of the night next day. The following suggestions may help:

1. You observe a specific object on one day and again on the next, and you see a great deal the second time which you either did not notice or misinterpreted previously.
2. You notice that on the second day the same object or theme has become more familiar, more personal and is accompanied by new feelings. It has become a little more a part of yourself.
3. By focussing on digesting what was there the day before, we can better experience the night-time corrections, improvements and new insights the next day.
4. This process can sometimes produce dramatic effects and even disturb our sleep. Something tells us: 'I was totally mistaken', 'Now I know what it is', 'That is the solution'. Day-time learning blockages do not function at night, so decisive breakthroughs become possible. The adult educator must learn how to use questions that will make the participants aware of these experiences and then help them integrate them as constructively as possible in their learning process.
5. It is very important to notice how day-time efforts with regard to learning blockages are metamorphosed during the night into improvements and in the long run also into capabilities and skills. Improvements are noticeable the very next day. The adult educator must make a great effort in connection with these encouraging experiences. These learning blockages can teach him to love and to understand that such learning is only possible on the earth because of the hindrances earthly existence brings with it. Capabilities can only unfold as a result of these hindrances.

6. The manner in which you learn during the day has an important influence on night-time processes. In this connection it is very important that the three learning paths intermingle and strengthen one another. Only when they combine do spiritual growth and the continuous renewal of your being of spirit and soul come about. You regularly assess how much progress you have made in day-time and night-time learning.

In order to support the night-time learning process at this stage the following three very profound questions asked at the end of the day can be helpful:

I. What essential thing have I learnt today?

II. What is its significance for my future destiny?

III. What does it tell me about my spiritual path?

Next morning at the moment of waking you can receive very important indications. The schooling task here is to grasp hold of these before they disappear as the first sense impressions of the day take hold. You discover that the human being knows much more than he is intellectually aware of.

7. This step of day-time and night-time learning is very difficult to describe because the creative element appears at the border between conscious day-time learning and unconscious night-time learning. Waking up and falling asleep alternate like two ways of crossing a threshold. The creative point reached by the adult educator is when he achieves a balance between the two learning processes. He must neither descend into rigid routine nor float off in unfocussed flurries of activity. The question to be asked concerns the extent to which he can make his own schooling in day-time and night-time learning fruitful in assisting others.

To imbue the six Professional Fields with the seven learning processes in the manner described here could constitute one way in which the adult educator might tackle his schooling path independently. In this way the seventh Professional Field itself would also continuously be schooled. An adult educator schooling would then be able to awaken appropriate learning processes in every learning situation.

A musician once told me: 'When I miss out on one day's practice I notice it. I notice it even more when I miss out on two days' practice. When I don't practise for three days, my audience notices it!' The situation is exactly the same for the adult educator. Let this be our schooling motto!

*

Finally we should stress that self-education can be immeasurably strengthened and deepened for the adult educator if a number of colleagues join forces to practise a form of learning together. A group of this kind enables questions to be asked, experiences to be exchanged and exercises to be carried out. Most important of all is the mutual and constructive evaluation of each other's way of teaching. In adult learning one needs adult colleagues with whom to share one's independent self-education.

4. General Schooling of the Adult Educator

A few general points are listed below.

1. It is not a good idea to set up a programme lasting several years such as is customary for most professions nowadays, since this could lead to new professional deformations. What is needed are short intensive courses lasting from one week to a maximum of three months. These should alternate with practice periods in the field. Experience gained in practice and in seminars should be interrelated and equally balanced.
2. Since adult education is the matter in hand one good method would be for the participants to learn how to teach one another during their seminars. For example the course leaders might embark on a Destiny Learning exercise with a few of the participants who would then have to teach the same thing to the others. Many learning elements of the course would be suited to this kind of mutual education.
3. Although the three learning paths have to be developed separately because the steps are so different it is nevertheless important that the essence of all three should be present in every teaching session. Every learning situation has elements of destiny and also requires an attitude of mind involving research.
4. The course should include specific project work as well as specific research work.
5. Course leaders and participants can continuously practise the three ways in which adult educator and participants relate to one another (Part Three, 1). This relationship can then progress to ever higher levels.
6. Learning through practice, the schooling of abilities and the generation of a basic moral attitude should imbue all the course activities continuously and equally.
7. The participants should already be in possession of specialist knowledge and experience so that the course can

concentrate entirely on preparing them for the profession of adult educator.
8. Finally, everything that has been said before about the schooling of the adult educator could be transposed into a general course for adult educators.

These few incomplete suggestions will have to suffice, in the hope that one day, together with adult educators experienced in this field, it will be possible to bring into existence a general course for adult educators.

**Part Four:
Practical Applications**

The following seven essays describe some of the applications that can demonstrate how the seven Professional Fields are continuously on the move and possess tremendous variety.

It is hoped that these contributions will encourage the reader to tread new paths so that the Professional Fields may be increasingly enriched and deepened.

The author is most grateful to those who have contributed six of these essays (the seventh being one of his own). Their work shows that there are already a good number of adult educators working towards a renewal of adult learning in the sense described in this book.

1. Human Encounter
by Shirley Routledge

Creating the conditions that make human encounter possible

One of the fields the adult educator has to develop is the capacity for encounter. This is immensely important for facilitating Destiny Learning, and even more so for a helping conversation or individual counselling. The group work of Destiny Learning is only possible in a sphere of unconditional acceptance and trust between people. It seems that human encounter lies at the root of this work.

During many encounter exercises it was studied what furthered and what hindered truly human encounter. Slowly the following seven ego activities emerged as conditional for this process. This has been drawn from nine years of experience in the Anthroposophical Schooling Course (UK), in workshops on Destiny Learning, as well as from experiences in helping conversations with karma as background. The seven ego activities were put into practice during a course for counsellors in 1997 at Der Quellhof, Kirchberg, Germany.

For our research in encounter we addressed our question to the element of warmth as it permeates the space between people in human relationships. We differentiated body, soul and spirit warmth substance. The spirit warmth meant here is the substance created by a particular ego activity and in which our ego lives. With ego activity is meant an activity as an original, freely engendered ego act—not a reaction, or relating, or similar psychological processes. The ego is called on to be ever more centred and alive, objectively and lovingly interested in the destiny of each individual, on a level where personal sympathies and antipathies are irrelevant. Our personal responses become signals of our own karmic constitution which makes a true encounter possible or impossible.

172 PRACTICAL APPLICATIONS

The seven activities formed themselves into a seven-step process of encounter. Once familiar, the steps can be used more freely and artistically according to the situation, and eventually become faculties or a way of being that shines out in one's humanness.

The seven ego-activities

The first 3 steps are mainly preparation, creating the conditions. Steps 4 to 6 are the encounter itself, and step 7 the continuous process. All can be related to qualities of the sun.

1. Perceive and *acknowledge* the other person in the present moment with *full acceptance*, unconditionally, without prejudice or judgement or expectations. 'It is as it is and cannot be otherwise at this moment.'

This acceptance, offering your being as a clear, undistorted mirror for the other, gives the strength to be who one is with open honesty.

As the sunlight rays and shines for everything, and does not distinguish between saints and sinners, nor beautiful or ugly, true or untrue, so also the encountering person radiates as the sun itself.

2. Direct your attention to perceiving in a selfless way, using all twelve senses, *observing* the other person *with real interest* in his uniqueness in every detail and aspect. This requires withholding one's own reactions, irritations, associations, memories, sympathetic sentiments, etc., replacing subjective activity with an open empathy for how it is to be 'in his shoes'.

The picture nature of the other enters our awareness, and it is clear that the first step made this possible.

One can call this a refined breathing process through the senses. With every sense perception the spirit behind the outer appearance is also unconsciously streaming through us. The sun spirit observes us through the senses; a sun quality lives in every sensing process. When our heart is sensing and listening openly, the first impression of the karmic gesture of the other enters our awareness.

(This faculty is developed in the schooling of observation as in the Anthroposophical Schooling Course, UK.)

3. The first and second steps were focussed toward the other person. In step 3 you yourself are fully there. This means *being actively present in your most authentic self*, discarding roles, reactions, protections, or superficial behaviour. Relating to the other begins out of the courage to be as fully present as possible, with your own karmic composition. Being fully there and 'real' also gives the other courage to be present in so far as he is able to in this moment—but this may not be demanded or expected. You can only be responsible for your own ego activity.

'I carry the sun in me. He leads me as a King through the world.' The sun carries karma; it is in the spiritual sun realm that our karma is made consequent and our destiny for the next life prepared. Thus through the 'sun in me' you bring your old karma into the encounter, with all its pre-birth intentions and what you have so far become. You place yourself in the situation you prepared.

(In the night during sleep the moral after-image of our deeds is clearly visible to one another. You will know whether the lovely words someone spoke to you were real, filled with ego integrity, or merely sentimental soul comfort.)

4. *Ego activity now creates an 'open space' between us.* In step 3 we filled the space between us with our being; now we create the encounter space. Interest and attention shifts from the other person to what happens in the open space between us where both can appear. Our karma now weaves into the space, as echo of the sun sphere where we were together before birth.

This can be a very uncertain, 'emptiness' experience—one has no security or control. If there is silence between us, this has also to be filled with the warmth of active presence, not passivity or mere waiting (in which case you have stepped out, and the other cannot stay without you). One must not dominate or want to fill the space, but be ready to give of oneself to serve whatever wants to come about. The tendency is to fall back on past experiences, or what we already know, and bring this in—but this can sever contact; you are back in yourself and outside the present moment.

The best faculty for this is a heart-feeling-sensing-listening into the situation, a faculty that can sense processes, qualities and gestures. It is a refined feeling that is not an emotional response but a sensing discernment of what lives in the moment and what it asks of you. (Development of this is very much helped by artistic processes, calling on our aesthetic judgement.)

In the centre of the sun is less than nothing—a counterspace. We could expect this to implode on itself if there were not a force there that holds it. Rudolf Steiner described this as the spiritual centre of the sun, where spiritual beings of the second hierarchy have their existence. This fourth step could be called a social sun space.

5. Having created the space, nothing further can happen unless we *invest something of ourselves into the open space.* You act, and create new destiny according to how both are engaged actively. The ego can choose to take responsibility for acting in a way that may be fruitful into the future. There is always a risk involved because it should have the character of a free deed. You may be required to enter with empathy into the other's feelings, or questions, or shadows, or relationships to life—to go with what is necessary in the moment. You may need to withhold in order to affirm the other, giving and serving what is needed without imposing your own will or agenda. It is always a unique situation and therefore has nothing to do with our usual ways of relating to people, but should be a creative act.

When the inner 'sun' or ego being is allowed to shine out, both can recognize who they truly are, by reflecting the differences and what each asks from the other.

6. All the foregoing is preparation for the moment of *recognition* when like a flash you glimpse the true being of the other person. You may intuit why this person has to live within this karmic reality in this incarnation. Out of the recognition, destiny language may be spoken.

The light of day dawns! A ray of recognition by another confirms the ego in its will to live and create. Only by recognition by another can you know yourself, transform what hangs on from the past, or know the direction of your life intention. It is this recognition we all hope for. It comes as a grace and is not the totality, but as much as can be perceived at the moment.

These three ego acts (4, 5 and 6) can be done only for moments. They cannot be held indefinitely unless a rhythmic process is created that embraces all three.

7. A *breathing rhythmic movement* of encountering takes place, the ego actively offering itself to the other or withdrawing into itself. *When to reach out, when to withhold ...* When this is honestly done, past and future karma is held in balance so that the reality of the present can be found, and a person is strengthened for taking next steps out of his own responsibility and in freedom. A healing, helping process can emerge.

The sun quality of movement, systole/diastole, creates space and fills space. Centre and periphery relate and interweave.

Summary of the seven ego activities

Accept the other as he is
See the other as he is
You appear as you are
You create a counter-space in which we are
You act in the space in which we are
You experience something of the being of the other
You move rhythmically in and out of the encounter space.

Out of spirit-ego-fire we can have interest in and acknowledgment for every human being. We do not have to like the other, or agree with him, but we can recognize him and give him the spiritual freedom to be who he is. These encounter steps are beyond soul processes—they have deed character.

In practice most people realized they could not produce

these qualities at random since many blockages, fears and insecurities played a role. Nevertheless when carried as a serious endeavour the steps already showed a positive effect and were for both persons a unique experience.

In the schooling for the 'encountering conversation' at Der Quellhof, these seven ego activities were practised daily for one week, in conversations with a partner. Both persons then evaluated together which ego activities they were able to achieve and which were under-developed. The ego activities were also practised in artistic exercises, in conversations in colour (chalk pastel), to follow the steps and explore what was being experienced and what was being asked of each person. The artistic exercises also had the aim of developing aesthetic sensitivity, and the feeling-sensing faculties for being present in the moment. 'Sense of ego' exercises were also introduced on the first day of the week to explore levels of encounter. In later work with clients it was reported that a therapeutic force could be observed emanating from these seven ego activities. This indicates that true encounter can be an act of healing.

I see this spirit fire and sun space as essential to resolve the social problems of our time and to move into the future with creative human forces.

2. Judgement Forming—a Dynamic Model
by Lex Bos

1. Introduction

When you listen to people talking you realize that most of what they are telling each other amounts to an exchange of judgements. They have opinions about everything: whether something works well or not, whether something is beautiful or ugly, whether something is good or not. Usually they also have opinions about who ought to do what in order to solve one problem or another.

All these judgements have created the reality in which we now live, and in future the world will continue to be determined by them.

If we are worried about this world in which we live we shall have to ask ourselves how the judgements that have formed it came about. Were they reached consciously and carefully? Could we be more careful and conscious? To find an answer we first need to ask what a judgement really is and how it comes about, and this will be our aim in the following pages.

2. The path of knowledge and the path of choice

Expressing a judgement is an inner activity, not a natural event taking place outside of us. Expressing a judgement is an inherent capability making itself felt within, which means that being capable of forming judgements is something we can learn to do.

To what do our judgements relate? What is this inner capability directed towards? Judgements can relate to the past or the future. If we feel the need to formulate our opinion about a situation our judgement relates to the past, and our activity is explorative. So we set out along what I shall call the 'path of knowledge'.

If we feel the need to formulate what ought to happen if a particular problem is to be solved, then our judgement relates to the future, and we set out along what I shall call the 'path of choice'.

Here is a summary in diagram form:

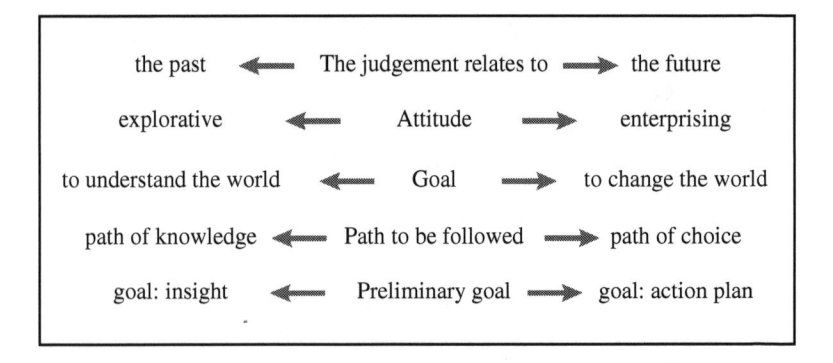

the past ←	The judgement relates to →	the future
explorative ←	Attitude →	enterprising
to understand the world ←	Goal →	to change the world
path of knowledge ←	Path to be followed →	path of choice
goal: insight ←	Preliminary goal →	goal: action plan

Our judgement can also relate to this very day, and in this case we are giving expression to what we are experiencing in the here and now. I shall return to this in Section 10.

In Section 5 I shall show how the two paths—the path of knowledge and the path of choice—relate to one another, how they need one another and how the conscious formulation of judgements constitutes a synthesis of both paths. But first I want to have a closer look at the two paths separately.

3. The path of knowledge: percepts and concepts

In the diagram the (preliminary) goal of the path is stated to be 'insight'. What happens when a physician finishes his examination of a patient with the conclusion: asthma. What happens when a management consultant attributes a steady slide into the red to a cash-flow problem? What occurs when a palaeontologist recognizes a few bones as belonging to a dinosaur? In each case a judgement is expressed in the form of 'This is ...' or 'What is happening here is ...'. The essential element is that we are talking about a relationship between a

Judgement Forming—a Dynamic Model

percept of something that is outside ourself and a concept (or a set of concepts, a theory, a hypothesis) that we carry within us. We have selected the relevant concepts by means of our own activity from amongst those available to us.
We cannot see concepts, but we can think them. The concept 'chair' is invisible; it embraces an infinite number of possible chairs. In our inner landscape of concepts the concept 'chair' stretches from a footstool to an armchair. If we see an object in the externally perceptible world that fits one of our concepts, the inner picture 'chair', 'footstool', 'armchair' takes shape within us. We discover our concept in external reality and express this by saying: 'That is a chair.' Our ability to form judgements can also be applied to much more complicated percepts: a difficult conflict situation, a complex problem, a puzzling illness with contradictory test results. The concept-systems we draw on can also be more complicated. But the process of forming a judgement remains basically the same, and consists of relating one percept to one concept.

In ordinary talk, expressing a judgement is thought to be the same as expressing an opinion: 'I like that', 'I didn't think that was a nice thing to do', 'This makes me feel threatened'. Such expressions are in fact incomplete judgements, not mature ones. The statement expresses a relationship, but it is a relationship between the speaker and an external phenomenon. This emotional relationship can block our ability to reach a genuine judgement. The statement says more about the speaker than about what has happened, and thus has the character of a prejudice. This emotional relationship can, though, also provide an opening in the direction of the 'path of knowledge' if the speaker succeeds in making the feeling judgement objective with regard both to the percept and the choice of concept. On the other hand the emotional relationship can also provide an opening in the direction of the 'path of choice' if the speaker realizes that his emotions originate in specific intentions or future expectations. Judgements along the path of knowledge can also arise by relating two concepts.

180 PRACTICAL APPLICATIONS

Philosophically, the formulation 'The human being is a mammal' is a knowledge judgement, even though no percepts lead to this formulation. A narrower concept is applied in the framework of a wider one. The activity of knowledge is actually related to or identical with relating a narrower percept to a wider concept.

4. The path of choice: goals and means

Finding a judgement via the path of choice also involves a formulation concerning a relationship. Having set his sights on certain goals, an entrepreneur looks for ways and means of achieving them. In the diagram at the end of Section 2 the term 'action plan' indicates the goal of the path of choice. It expresses the judgement: 'These are the means by which we can achieve these goals, these goals fit the means and the means are adequate for the task of reaching the goals.' In his judgements on the path of choice the entrepreneur expresses the relationship between goals and means. There can be many variations of this relationship, as expressed in the following extreme examples:

— Shooting midges with canon is an activity in which the means are out of all proportion to the goal.
— Emptying the ocean with a spoon is an activity in which the goal is out of all proportion to the means.
— When we say that the goal sanctifies the means we are stating that the means do not fit the goal, or are even unworthy of it.
— When we say that the means demean the goal we are stating that we have been tempted to depict something inappropriate as the goal merely in order to have an opportunity to employ certain means.

In formulating our judgement along the path of choice we encounter the same phenomenon of inside/outside as on the path of knowledge. In the latter case we spoke of percepts taken from outside and concepts searched for and formed by inner activity. On the path of choice the goals are inside and the means outside. Within an organization the employees are often given their goals from outside, for example by their boss, and the goals usually concern matters to be achieved in the outside world, but nevertheless, the goals themselves originate inside a human being. When we warm to certain goals, when we decide to follow a specific direction in the future, when we feel enthusiastic about an ideal or about certain moral values, this is an inner force. But when we search for the means by which to realize these goals it is in the outside world that we must look around. That is where we shall find the materials, the people, the organizational forms, the legal framework and so on which can help us along the path towards our goal.

When we formulate a judgement in ordinary talk we are not merely stating our opinion about a situation (as shown in Section 3) but we are also expressing what we think ought to happen: 'I think things ought to go in such and such a direction', 'I don't think they'll reach their goal by this means', 'I find these goals unrealistic'. Such expressions are in fact incomplete judgements, not mature ones. Again we recognize this fact because the formulation refers to a relationship, the relationship between oneself and the future. Again this emotional relationship can block our ability to reach a genuine judgement. The statement says more about the speaker than about the future and thus has the character of a prejudice. This emotional relationship can, though, also provide an opening in the direction of the path of choice if the speaker succeeds in making the feeling judgement objective with regard both to the goals and the means. On the other hand the emotional relationship can also provide an opening in the direction of the path of knowledge if the speaker realizes that his emotions originate in specific experiences and their interpretation. Judgements along the path of choice can also influence the relationship between the goals. Just as individual concepts are a part of our landscape of concepts with its superior, equal and subordinate concepts, so do goals not stand by themselves but remain always a part of a complex of goals comprising superior and subordinate partial goals. Creating order in this landscape of goals is another activity of a human being who is set on the path of choice. It is an activity that is related to, or even identical with, relating means to goals.

5. Foreground and background

In studying the process by which we reach judgements I have so far distinguished between two paths each of which has two areas. The path of knowledge has the areas of percepts and concepts, and the path of choice those of goals and means.

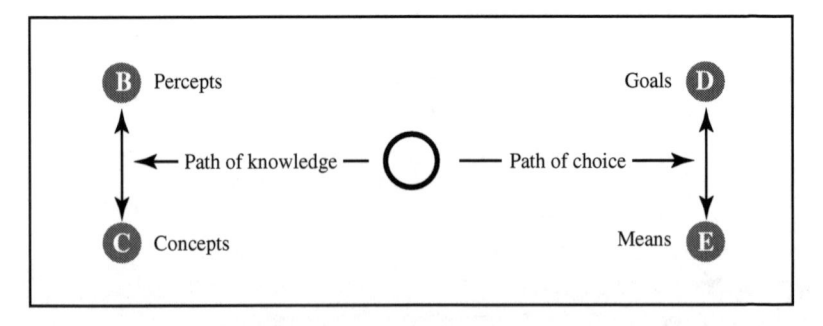

```
    B  Percepts                          Goals  D
       ↑                                   ↑
       ← Path of knowledge ─ O ─ Path of choice →
       ↓                                   ↓
    C  Concepts                           Means  E
```

For simplicity's sake in the diagram the areas are designated by letters. These have no meaning as such and their sequence is also irrelevant. Each simply denotes one area, which could be described in many ways:

B stands for percepts, facts, observations, data, information, experience, events, examples, descriptions etc.
C stands for concepts, characteristics, thoughts, theories, hypotheses, drafts, thought models, laws, ideas etc.
D stands for goals, intentions, wishes, desires, decisions, values, ideals, motives, impulses etc.
E stands for ways and means, procedures, tools, methods, practices, facilitations, resources etc.

In this Section I shall investigate the connections between the paths and the connections between the areas. Can each exist alone, or do they need one another?

Judgement Forming—a Dynamic Model

Take a researcher. His is primarily the path of knowledge and superficially you might think that he has nothing to do with the path of choice. But this is not the case. Originally he formulated his research goal and, for example, he also decided which method of investigation he would employ. He also made sure of having certain means at his disposal (time, money, lab space and so on). While these activities were going on the path of choice took centre stage, while the path of knowledge still remained in the background.

Having concluded his preparations on the path of choice the researcher then begins his investigations. The paths swop places as required. When the path of knowledge comes to the fore, the path of choice recedes. These positions may remain for some time, perhaps until funds begin to run short, or the researcher has second thoughts about his chosen method, or even if his motivation flags. Then the path of choice re-emerges while the path of knowledge disappears into the background as the researcher turns his attention to the goals and methods of his research.

The case of an entrepreneur is similar. His attention is primarily directed towards the path of choice. He sets himself goals, selects the means, and is busy in many directions. Nevertheless the path of knowledge is also involved, although it does not appear in the foreground. It remains in the background and takes the form of all kinds of ideas the entrepreneur has about the real situation and how to develop it, ideas about his own business, the market situation, his competitors, trade unions, politics and so on.

But then the real situation turns out to be unexpectedly different. The entrepreneur is suddenly inundated by complaints. Why is his product no longer successful? Where has his motivation gone? These are all questions that make him turn his attention to the path of knowledge and push the path of choice temporarily into the background, until new points of departure can be found for his renewed activity, at which point his attention turns once more towards the path of choice. So in this case too the path of knowledge and the path of choice alternate, with one appearing in the foreground while the other recedes into the background.

The same thing happens on a smaller scale within each path. On the path of knowledge our consciousness is ordinarily rather more aware of sense-impressions, which thus occupy the foreground. We are less aware of the way all these impressions are accompanied by concepts that turn what we perceive into inner pictures; but this is not yet a matter of forming judgements consciously. A change takes place when we are confronted by percepts that we do not understand. This will trigger an alternation between periods of heightened attention to sense-perceptions ('What exactly are we looking at? What is this?') and concentration on the search for and formulation of relevant concepts ('Is it a shooting star or a satellite?'). Percepts and concepts alternate with each other in coming to the fore and retreating to the background.

This alternation happens likewise on the path of choice. There is a great deal of routine in everyday life; we have already decided how to do things and our goals are obvious, so we do not really have to form judgements consciously. This changes when we are thwarted in what we are doing or when our actions fail to have the desired outcome. A process of judgement forming begins in which we alternately ask ourselves 'What are we actually doing?' and 'Why are we doing this; what is our motivation; what is our goal?' When one of these questions comes to the fore the other does not disappear. It merely recedes, only to come forward again at a later stage.

The conclusion I hope the reader will draw from the above is that the model depicted here is holistic.

Both paths and all four areas are present at the same time in every judgement forming process. Both paths and all four areas are needed if a conscious decision is to be made. The two paths are complementary, the four areas are complementary in pairs. During the process of judgement forming they come to the fore alternately, whereby the other half in each pair then momentarily retires into the background.

While this judgement forming model is holistic, the judgement forming process is rhythmical. This should already have become obvious in principle. In the following Section I shall endeavour to make it more concrete.

6. Forming judgements in phases or as a dialogue?

It is extremely important to question the type of process used in forming judgements because the type of process determines the type of outcome. If the process of judgement forming follows a mechanistic, logical, causal line in which every step follows the preceding one and prepares the following one with rigid regularity, then it is likely that the insights and action plans that form the conclusion of this process will not stand up to the requirements of real life. To find answers that are appropriate for real life a different method is needed, as becomes all too obvious when we look at the results of the causal, logical, linear, mechanistic approach so often applied in our present time (e.g. in matters of environment, health, education and so on).

In the previous Section we suggested that rhythm is essential in the process of forming judgements, rather than the causal, linear, dead factors found in inanimate nature. Rhythm is a matter of living processes, and I shall now look at this more closely.

The process on the path of knowledge usually begins in area B with a percept we do not understand. Almost immediately our thinking throws up a concept, a hypothesis, a possible theoretical explanation: 'Is it a beech tree? Has the patient got asthma? Has the second stage in conflict escalation already taken place?' As we examine the possibilities we are in area C when we ask ourselves: 'If it's a beech tree the bark should have specific characteristics. If it's asthma the patient should be showing certain symptoms. If the second stage has occurred there should be other phenomena as well.' These considerations send us back to area B to look for more data in support of our hypothesis. Perhaps we shall find some, in which case our initial intuitive thought was correct. But more often our renewed, improved perception reveals new phenomena which oblige us to look for new concepts, to adapt our hypothesis or correct our theory. In short, our activities necessitate a return to area C, after which we have to assess our findings once more in area B. This goes on until we are satisfied. It is a rhythmical process, or we might also call it a dialogue. B and C converse with one another, they ask each other questions and provide the answers. When they have reached agreement the investigator is (provisionally) content.

The path of choice at first appears to follow a logical, linear process. Surely it is logical to be clear about one's goals before being able to think meaningfully about how to reach them. The sequence is obvious, and a phase-model appears to be in order: begin with area D and move on to E. However, this assumption turns out to be mistaken, for in fact it is not at all easy to be clear about area D.

Area D has to do with impulses, intentions, future options, and these for their part originate in our will which it is not at all easy for us to approach consciously. So it turns out that we shall have to use area E in order to become fully aware of what area D entails.

Nevertheless, the path of choice is usually embarked on via area D. We want to solve a problem, settle a dispute or, oriented more positively towards the future, manufacture environmentally friendly products or find ways of allowing members (of a society, for example) to share more directly in decision-making, and so on. Very soon we find ourselves in area E with questions as to how this might be realized in practice. We work out scenarios. These produce concrete ideas about what the realization of the original goals might lead to. In the light of this future prospect we then ask: 'Is this really what we want? Does this satisfy us?' These questions in area D make us rethink and reformulate our goals, after which we have to return to area E in order to find new ways and means. These new ways and means also have their consequences, for example an unexpected dependence on specific groups, personal sacrifice, the obligation to acquire new capabilities. We must want these consequences. We begin to realize that the goals we originally formulated are a part of a larger landscape of goals the whole of which we must want.

So once again we return to area D as we work on becoming more aware, reflect on the matter and re-formulate our goals yet again, after which renewed activity in area E becomes necessary. This process continues until we have developed our action plan in which goals and means are sufficiently clarified and satisfactorily harmonized with one another. The process has once again been largely rhythmical and like a dialogue.

At this point let us turn to the overall process that includes both the path of knowledge and the path of choice. Virtually all the available literature on problem solving and decision making describes this process as having phases. Apart from the preliminary phase of stating the problem (to which I shall return in the next Section), all the current models are variations of the basic one: image building—judgement forming—decision making. There are always three consecutive steps. In the light of what we have been saying here, the image of the situation is reached at the end of the path of knowledge. The facts have become an image because one's thinking has ordered them and made them transparent. Arriving at this type of image is the end result of an intensive process of judgement forming.

In fact, however, postponing judgement forming until after the image has been built means that no image has actually been built at all; there has merely been a gathering of information. If the term judgement forming in this three-phase model is taken to mean a stage when those taking part are allowed to let their feelings run free, describe their own experience of the situation, give their opinions about it and so on, then these feelings can either be used as the entry into a contribution in the knowledge process, or they can be included as facts to be considered in area B! In neither case is there any justification for having a separate judgement forming phase after image building (path of knowledge).

The same applies to the path of choice. The action plan as the final stage of the path of choice is the result of an intensive judgement forming process. But if no more judgements were to be allowed after the judgement forming phase, an action plan would never materialize. If the intention in the three-phase model is for feelings to be expressed in this phase with regard to goals and possible solutions, then the same has to be said about this as was said above regarding image building. The feelings can either be used to deepen the judgement forming process on the path of choice, or they must be included among the ideas formed about the consequences of specific solutions. In neither case is there any justification for having a separate judgement forming phase prior to decision making (path of choice).

The first conclusion to be drawn from this consideration of the three-phase model is that it disintegrates into a two-phase model. Instead of image building, judgement forming and decision making, it becomes path of knowledge / path of choice. Judgement forming as a separate middle phase is omitted or, in other words, the whole process becomes a single continuum of judgement (re)forming!

Let us look more closely at the phases. In the path of knowledge / path of choice model one can also talk of two phases: the path of knowledge must be trodden first, before one is allowed to embark on the path of choice. It is not easy to evade the logic of this sequence: first the diagnosis, then the therapy; first analyse the problem, then take measures to tackle it. Is it perhaps after all a matter of a linear phase model and not a dialogue? No! Dialogues are involved in various ways.

Let us begin with the purely diagnostic conversation. Its purpose is solely to grasp what the patient is suffering from, what the matter is with the child, why the organization is failing. The path of choice is not active in the sense of finding solutions; it is as it were contained within the path of knowledge. The purpose (D) is to carry on this conversation with the intention of doing so by adhering to the rules of group dynamics and content (E). The dialogue is then carried along in a rhythmical alternation between conducting the conversation (B/C) and reflecting thereon in keeping with the previously formulated intentions (D) and the agreed method (E). The two need each other. The goals and means are more or less realized through the conversation. And the conversation itself can be enriched and deepened through reflection on this.

When the conversation reaches the point of becoming a discussion about solutions and therefore enters explicitly upon the path of choice, the dialogue between path of knowledge and path of choice gains two new ways of coming to expression. On the one hand the solutions must be constantly checked against the situation. As a result, aspects of the situation enter the conversation that were not yet relevant when the patient (or the child or the organization) was being discussed. Now, as though one were still on the path of knowledge, it is a matter of investigating whether specific solutions are possible and can be realized financially, technically, legally, politically and so on. On the other hand, only when the participants begin to formulate the goals and means does it become clear how various are their estimations of the situation, their interpretations of the diagnosis, their reading of the picture. The situation is like that in the example mentioned earlier, in which the goals only become conscious when the means are made concrete. In the present case entirely new diagnostic questions arise on the path of choice, necessitating a return to the path of knowledge.

We have now discovered three types of dialogue between the path of knowledge and the path of choice: the dialogue between the path of knowledge and its own 'inner realm'; the dialogue between the path of choice and a much wider realm of image building; and the dialogue in the narrower sense between path of choice and path of knowledge. These dialogues in turn relate to one another in dialogue fashion. They cannot be treated sequentially in phases. They need one another and mutually determine the quality of the judgement forming process.

So there is no way in which the path of knowledge, the path of choice or a mutual path combining both can be seen as a phase model. From the very outset judgement forming is a rhythmical process of dialogue.

7. The central position of the question

Thus far I have defined the paths and within these the areas, and I have shown that the judgement forming process is one not of linear phases but of rhythmical dialogue. I have not as yet sought to clarify what gives the process its dynamic and its direction. The answer is as simple as it is basic. What moves and guides the process is: a question. Every active process of judgement forming is founded on a question. Those who do not want to grasp the world or change it through their activity are content with themselves and with the world; at most they will say what they think of it or what ought to be changed. An active process of judgement forming only begins when questions come alive. These can manifest as 'knowledge questions' when we are dissatisfied with ourselves ('I want to understand the world'), or as 'choice questions' when we are dissatisfied with the world ('I want to change the world'). Knowledge questions provide us with the strength to tread the path of knowledge and guide us as we move along it. Choice questions give us the strength to tread the path of choice and guide us as we move along it.

As a dialogue proceeds, knowledge questions can be so precise as to become specific B or C questions ('What actually happened?' 'What does this concept denote?'). Similarly choice questions can become specifically D or E questions ('What exactly is our goal now?' 'How should we picture this path?'). It is important to understand that every question has to have an originator. Who the originator is can be discovered by asking questions like: 'Who is asking this question? Who is particularly concerned with this question? Who is lying awake at night thinking about this question? Who genuinely wants to find an answer to this question?' If there is no clear answer to these enquiries we can be sure that the judgement forming process will follow a colourless, weak course in which no one is particularly interested. The results will be correspondingly disappointing.

The first step in the phase model cited above is the question. This is followed by image building, judgement forming and decision making. Then it becomes obvious that this model is not very realistic. We all know how questions change as we go along. A new question is discovered behind or beneath the original one, a detail becomes dominant, or the entire problem suddenly shifts to a different position. In fact the most important result of a conversation is often the discovery and formulation of the real question.

So the question is now at the end and not the beginning. Frequently once the real question has appeared the answer follows immediately.

Actually the question is present both at the beginning and at the end, and along the path in between as well. Working on the question, checking it and reformulating it are activities that run through the whole conversation. In fact this process, also, is like a rhythmical dialogue. It is a conversation between the (changing) question and the (growing) answer.

8. The lemniscate as a symbol

The lemniscate is a good symbol for the judgement-forming process we have been describing. The word is Greek and denotes the garland of flowers received by a victor on his return from battle. The garland surrounded his head, crossed over in the heart region and its lower loop encompassed the abdomen (Fig. 1).

Mathematicians use the lemniscate as a symbol for infinity.

We can use it in our present context because:

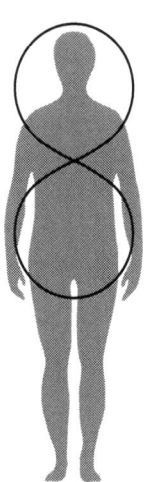

Figure 1

— it shows a continuous process with no beginning and no end. Judgement forming processes always begin with existing judgements and have a provisional conclusion. In this sense they are infinite in that they have no beginning and no end.

192 PRACTICAL APPLICATIONS

— it represents a process of dialogue between inner and outer. What is inside in the left-hand loop is outside in the right-hand loop, and vice versa (Fig. 2).

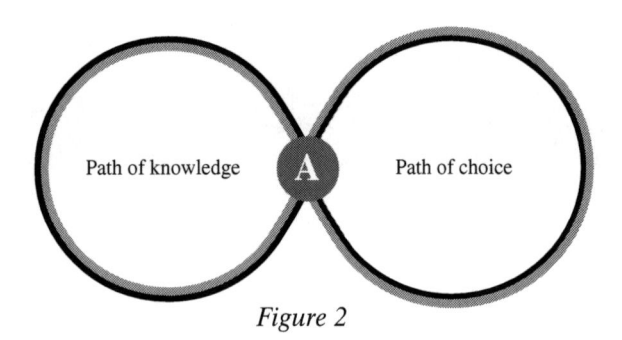

Figure 2 — Path of knowledge — A — Path of choice

On the path of knowledge the result is inside us (a learning process, understanding the world). On the path of choice it is outside us (changing the world). On the path of knowledge the percepts are outside us and the thoughts inside (Fig. 3). On the path of choice the will impulses are in us and the means outside (Fig. 4). It is extremely important for the judgement forming process to have a clear centre from which the dialogue can commence and to which it can return. In this centre (see Fig. 2) we have placed the human being with his question ('A'). It is indeed this human being with his question who directs the whole dialogue.

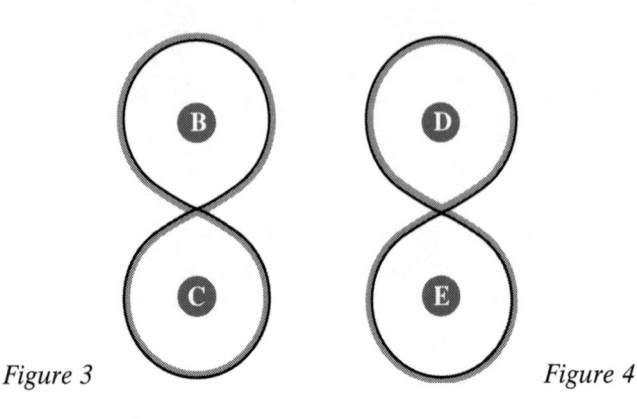

Figure 3 (B, C)   *Figure 4* (D, E)

9. The importance of feeling

When we try to imagine our inner life in the form of a map we discover three provinces there. The first comprises inner pictures, thoughts and memories; the second feelings, emotions and experiences; the third desires, intentions and will impulses. To paraphrase these they could be termed 'thinking, feeling and will'. The outside world enters us in the form of percepts, while our inner world enters the outside world in the form of actions.

The description thus far might have given the impression that feeling has no place in the judgement forming process. The path of knowledge addresses thinking (and perceiving), while the path of choice addresses the will (actions). Feelings have so far been categorized either as preliminary steps leading up to the forming of an actual judgement in both the path of knowledge and the path of choice, or as facts to be included in areas B or E. Are we thus underrating the value of feeling? This question brings us to a remarkable paradox, for in fact the inmost core of the judgement forming process is connected with feeling. Feeling is a faculty that enables us to express the relationship one thing has with another: how fact relates to norm, how shapes, colours and sounds relate amongst each other, how human beings behave towards each other and, finally, how we ourselves relate to all this. Even the judgement itself expresses a relationship: how a thought relates to a percept, a means to a goal, the past to the future.

The paradox is that precisely because the judgement forming process is essentially an activity of feeling we have to be extremely careful how we give our everyday feeling (burdened as it is with subjective sympathies and antipathies, prejudices and desires) the place it deserves in this process. Feeling needs to undergo a long path of development before it can be used in the process of forming judgements. The way in which I have described this process includes hints as to where feeling can be schooled. We encounter feeling in three places in the judgement forming process—and this is where it differs from forming judgements on the basis of feelings and subjective prejudices. These three places are: the motivation, the process and the result of judgement forming.

Motivation—process—result is a threefold time-beat in every human activity. The motivation frequently originates in unconscious depths and gives strength to the activity. In the process, activity appears as a sequence of actions taking place in time. The result stands still in space.

This threefold time-beat can, for example, be applied to someone who is learning (motivation for learning, learning process, learning result), or to someone who is conducting research (motivation for research, research method, research result), and to someone working (motivation for the work, work process, result of the work), and so on. The threefold time-beat helps us discover various aspects of an activity. One of the things it shows us is the role feeling plays in judgement forming:

— *The motivation* for forming a judgement. Behind the knowledge question and the choice question described above as being the source of strength for the process there is a feeling. Behind the knowledge question there is the feeling of astonishment and surprise (Plato knew that all science arises out of surprise). Behind the choice question there is an oppressive feeling of responsibility. Genuine knowledge and choice questions can arise from such feelings.
— *The process* of forming a judgement. Feeling can provide enlightenment about the quality of the process. Is it rushing chaotically from one of the four areas to another? Has it got stuck on the path of knowledge. Is it plumping for solutions too hastily? Is it getting hung up on the formulation of goals? Or is there a healthy forward movement that does justice to each focal point in turn?
— *The result* of forming a judgement. Once again feeling is the umpire deciding on the result of the judgement forming process. Do the participants feel that the facts have been sufficiently explained and understood? Have

they the feeling that the goals have been correctly employed as means? Do they feel that the action plans on the path of choice take sufficient account of the situation insights arrived at during the path of knowledge?

One frequently hears people say: 'I have a feeling that several facts have not yet been clarified sufficiently. I have a feeling that we shall not reach our goal by going in this direction.' And so on. Such feelings should be taken seriously, for they offer opportunities for deepening the process of judgement forming.

Via these three 'stages' feeling is stripped of its sympathies and antipathies that are so destructive socially. It is schooled into becoming what I should like to call 'an organ of perception and knowledge'. In the following Section I shall show that this can provide new points of departure for the relationships between individuals in a conversation group.

10. Forming judgements and forming groups

In my considerations here I have for the most part been describing judgement forming as an individual process, and the conclusions I have drawn are certainly valid in situations where a single individual is wrestling with questions alone.

However, the fact is that in many cases several people are involved in having to reach decisions together. Making decisions alone is both easier and more difficult. It is easier because one can move along without being contradicted. It is more difficult because it is harder to hold a conversation with oneself, to tackle one's own prejudices, to overcome one-sided viewpoints, or to put one's own hobby-horses away in the corner.

Whatever the case may be, if we are to tackle judgement forming in groups a new dimension comes into play: the formation of the group, the interrelationships within it, and the group process. Group formation and judgement formation are two sides of the same coin. When human beings speak with one another there is always a content aspect (they are talking about something: judgement forming) and a relationship aspect (something takes place between them: group forming). Over the years the social sciences have taken possession of these aspects along two different paths and have thus alienated them from one another.

The content aspect has become the object of a technocratic view in which the whole judgement forming process has been turned into a linear method of 'problem solving and decision making', as though there were no kind of relationship between those whom it concerns. The relationship aspect has become the object of 'group dynamics and sensitivity training', a method in which group processes become detached from the content dimension. People live in 'here and now' relationships. No account is taken of a path of knowledge and a path of choice. The one direction leads to a cold, programmed world, the other to a warm but exceedingly unrealistic and shadowy world.

The judgement forming process I have been describing here endeavours to work with the content aspect in such a way that the relationship aspect can be included in a new manner that enables it to be combined with the content aspect. There are four parts to this:

1. Systematic work with the four areas and questions generates a new interest in the contributions various individuals bring forward to 'fill up' those areas. This leads to a positive acceptance of the way people with all their weaknesses are connected with the different areas. Out of this a new sense of responsibility arises from the fact that these individuals are to some extent brought together by their weaknesses. Thus serious work on the dialogue between the areas and the paths awakens objective interest, willingness to accept, and responsibility for the human relationships. The areas and the paths show up the interpersonal relationships.
2. Since this judgement forming process treats feelings as organs of perception and knowledge, the feelings are purified of the sympathy and antipathy that are so

Judgement Forming—a Dynamic Model

destructive in relationships. The relationships thereby acquire a different content.
3. Instead of being rejected, 'feeling judgements' about content are taken seriously and used as a springboard for deepening the judgement forming process. In consequence, such 'feeling judgements' do not proliferate as undigested elements with a life of their own.
4. If it becomes necessary to talk about the relationships within the group, experience has shown that the lemniscate model provides a strong grip within the slippery and dangerous environment of 'talking about relationships', thus preventing the participants from slipping up or otherwise causing damage. Even here the group is concerned with a question and must therefore work through the four areas. The conversation remains 'clean' if this is adhered to.

When judgement forming improves group development in this way, the interrelationship becomes obvious. Improved relationships enhance the quality of the judgement forming process; the participants dare to express their opinions with more assurance and thus make themselves more vulnerable; they have the courage to leave some of their rationalizations on one side and address matters more directly and more personally. In this way judgement forming becomes more effective and deeper, which in turn strengthens the confidence the group members have in one another. This process of mutual strengthening between judgement forming and group development can also be regarded as a dialogue between the two, an interplay between the outer side of the events (the content being dealt with usually lies outside the group both in time and space) and the inner side of the same events (things that have to do with relationships take place in the 'here and now' within the group [see remark at the end of Section 2]).

A third basic attitude is now added to that of the investigator (on the path of knowledge) and the entrepreneur (on the path of choice), namely that of the one who is encountering others (in the realm of relationships). In addition to the knowledge question and the choice question we now have a third: the relationship question. 'Who is this other person? Is there something we have to do together?' Just as the knowledge question brings up feelings of surprise and the choice question feelings of oppression, so does the relationship question generate feelings of empathy, of being involved with others.

Now, at the end of this essay, I should like to describe the model I have been discussing as a 'social-ecological model', for the following reasons. The real purpose behind any agricultural activity is ecological; it involves cultivating a piece of the environment, a number of related environmental factors, so that something can grow. A farmer sows a seed, but he himself is not capable of making this seed grow into an ear of corn. He has to trust that the ear of corn is lying dormant as a potential within the seed. All he himself can do, to the best of his ability, is cultivate the environmental factors by providing sufficient minerals, water, air, light and warmth. He does not do this once and in a specific sequence. Throughout the whole growing season he applies each one again and again, as and when necessary.

This image is a realistic metaphor for the process of judgement forming in a group. When the seed of a question is planted in the soil of the group, the group members, like the farmer, are not able to produce the answer. They can only trust that the answer exists as a potential within the question-seed, waiting to be freed by correct environmental care: sufficient hard facts in area B; mobile, imaginative ways and means in area E; sufficiently clear thoughts in area C; and inspiring goals in area D. These social-ecological factors, too, are not applied in sequential phases, settled and done with once and for all. They are treated as and when necessary for the whole duration of the growth undergone by the answer to the original question. If this is done in a good way, then the potential answer lying dormant in the question-seed can be set free and harvested at the end of the conversation.

*

Judgement Forming—a Dynamic Model

The connection between what this essay has had to say about dynamic judgement forming and what the main book has described regarding the threefold process of judgement forming is surely obvious.

The path of knowledge is identical with the cognitive judgement process. Although the path of choice does not lead to an individual decision it does for the most part have the same orientation as the moral judgement process. The living, feeling human being 'A' stands at the centre, becoming aware of his relationship with the world in forming aesthetic judgements. He sends out his feelers to the left into the sphere of cognitive judgement and to the right into the sphere of moral judgement. All judgements originate in the centre.

When there are several 'A's at the centre, when judgement forming is carried out by a group, there is in the midst an autonomous process: group development. Here the relationships between human beings and their cognitive and moral judgements is central. The judgements that reign here are situational; they could be described as aesthetic.[1]

3. Some Exercises for Adult Learning and Destiny Learning
by C. J. van Houten

Experience has shown that learning exercises are much more effective if they are designed to include qualitatively different activities with a meaningful relationship to each other.

For example the group might begin by thinking around and into a core idea or question (a), after which they could compress it into a single sentence (b). Then they might speak this sentence clearly and with conviction (c). After that they could paint or model what they have spoken in this way (d), before finally returning once more to the beginning with the question: 'What does my picture or my clay figure express now?' (e). After this the whole progress of the idea can be traced backwards in order to discover more consciously how the development took place. A step by step enhancement of an idea using various media greatly deepens the learning process.

The separate activities can of course be varied. For example the sentence (b) could take the form of a short poem, the painting might also be expressed in a movement, or the modelled shape be transposed into music.

The adult educator must find the sequence that is appropriate to the learning aim that has been set. (We should remember that in adult learning the learning aim is always made known to the participants in advance, so that they can understand the purpose of the exercise.)

A further enhancement of the learning process in an exercise can be achieved by using polarities, for example considering two contrasting ideas such as 'untruth' and 'truth' or 'arrogance' and 'humility'. First the ideas are taken separately through the steps (a) to (d). Then they are brought face to face. The first sentence is spoken clearly and distinctly ('What is untruth?'). Then there is a short pause while the participants follow inwardly what happens as they prepare for the second sentence ('What is truth?'). This sentence is then spoken, after which there is another pause to allow the after-effects of both sentences to settle. Finally the participants exchange their experiences, which usually leads to a rich harvest of new viewpoints.

This exercise, minus the painting or modelling, has been applied in adult learning seminars to help the participants experience the sense of truth. A regular repetition of the same exercise enhances people's experience of truth. The exercise is described below in more detail. (The group should consist of five to six persons plus the adult educator.)

A. *'Untruth':*
(The participants work separately)

1. For about a quarter of an hour the participants consider what untruth really means for them personally. They look for two or three examples in their own biography which they have experienced either in themselves or in the world around them.
2. Each then compresses the result into a single sentence expressing the essence. The sentence is written down.
3. Each speaks the sentence to the group clearly and with conviction. One participant follows the next, so that five or six 'sentences about untruth' are heard.
4. The participants then have a brief exchange about what each has experienced.

B. *'Truth':*
The same four steps are then followed through with the concept 'truth', including two or three biographical examples.

C. *Now, following one another, the participants:*
1. speak the first sentence;
2. make a brief pause in which they observe inwardly how the adjustment to the second sentence takes place;
3. speak the second sentence;

4. make a brief pause to allow the after-effects of both sentences to settle.

Then the group briefly exchange their experiences of how the increased tension between the two polarities came about.

An observant adult educator who is familiar with Destiny Learning can sense how the karma forces begin to sound through this search for the truth. 'Platonists' and 'Aristotelians', for example, will express their relationship with the truth differently. Depending on the circumstances, and if appropriate, the adult educator can add his observations about the exercise.

*

Another version of this type of exercise is used in Destiny Learning. The learning aim is to assist in the transition from Learning Step IV, 'accepting one's own karmic being', to Learning Step V, 'practising in daily life'.

This exercise should only be undertaken as a part of the Destiny Learning process described in this book because the prerequisite for it is a sufficient measure of positivity, trust and openness in the group.

At the beginning of Learning Step V, here is the exercise for a group of four to six participants who have gone through the previous steps together:

A)

1. The participants endeavour to get to know their own 'karmic being' better by meditating on it for about 15 minutes, trying to visualize its attributes, its character, its movements and gestures. How does it behave? What are its colours and shapes? What form does it have?
2. They formulate this in a single sentence.
3. They write the sentence in the top left-hand corner of a sheet of paper, after which they use pastel chalks to draw it and let its shape become visible.

4. They speak the sentence aloud, show their picture to the group and discuss it.

B)

1. Now for about 15 minutes, on the basis of what has taken place, the participants meditate on newly visible or newly to be developed characteristics of their own.
2. They formulate what is new in a single sentence.
3. They write this sentence in the top right-hand corner of a sheet of paper, after which they use pastel chalks to make its colour and shape visible by drawing.
4. They speak the sentence aloud, show their picture to the group and discuss it.

C)

1. The participants now endeavour to paint the first being moving towards the second in such a way that something in between can arise. They try to make the second picture arise out of the first in as organic and artistic a way as possible.
2. Then the pictures (with titles) are shown to the group and discussed with them. As good a description as possible should be given of how the transformation of the one picture into the other is experienced.

First alternative: Another way of doing this would be to depict the transition physically by trying to move with gestures from the one to the other and then describing one's experiences while doing this.

Second alternative: Each participant can first go through the whole process alone before speaking the titles aloud and showing the pictures.

A subsequent discussion is possible in which practical suggestions can be given as to the best way of proceeding further in the practice of daily life.

4. The Seven Learning Steps in Painting Therapy
by Else Marie Henriksen

Some experiences in applying the seven learning processes in contemplating a picture during art therapy are described below as a further development of painting therapy.

There are two preconditions. Firstly the application of the seven learning processes to picture contemplation should only be undertaken with patients who have been having painting therapy for some time. Secondly, the painting chosen for consideration should contain elements that relate to the patient in question.

First step: Perceiving
First of all the picture is studied, which corresponds to the process of breathing in. A second stage is then introduced by the question: 'What am I seeing?' The patient now describes the picture as objectively and impersonally as possible, and this corresponds to the process of breathing out. In this first step the patient should relate to the picture as objectively as possible, going right into it. This can be difficult for someone who is ill.

Second step: Relating
In the first step the patient was asked to describe as accurately as possible what was to be seen in the picture. Now the pertinent question is 'Which aspect moves me most strongly? Are there parts of the picture to which I relate with sympathy or antipathy?' The patient has to relate to the picture personally and with feeling. He has to make a decision and learn to make a personal connection with something.

Third step: Digesting
This step is introduced by questions such as: 'Why am I moved by this particular part of the picture (which I picked

out myself in the previous step)? What do I experience in connection with it? What inner pictures or moods does it raise in addition?' The patient now has to work through and digest what he previously saw and took in. The therapist assists him in this by means of a helpful and sympathetic conversation, throwing light, for example, on biographical and karmic problem areas. Usually this progress through the learning steps brings the patient up against hindrances. For example a sudden realization may assail him when he comes to a point he has often reached before but which he now begins to see more clearly. In this situation the therapist must help him gain proper conscious insights.

Fourth step: Individualizing
The patient now contemplates the things he has worked through and experienced in the previous steps. This should lead to a realization of what the essential elements have been. The individualizing process can lead both to an 'Aha!' experience and/or to a painful one.

Fifth step: Practising
It is now time to find an exercise for the patient to practise daily so that the next two steps (*the sixth* 'developing new capabilities', and *the seventh* 'being creative and looking to the future') can follow. The exercise should enable the seed experiences and insights of the previous steps to grow. Then capabilities will also grow. Because of the individualization in the fourth step, there is greater motivation to practise, because the patient can see what good reasons there are to do so.

This learning path results in an increase in awareness and self-knowledge, and a growing ability to find one's way in life.

5. Adult Learning in Teaching Speech Formation
by Enrica dal Zio

We are only in the very early stages of applying the seven steps of adult learning in this field, but initial experience is very promising. A course usually involves developing a theme, something from literature, into which we enter and which we want to use as we learn speech formation. It may be a poem, a fairy tale, or anything else.

In the *first step* (breathing in for the participants) I read the text aloud and we then try to reproduce it together. The participants do this in their own words, striving to stay as close to the content and the author's or poet's manner of expression as possible (breathing out). In his lectures on speech formation[2] Rudolf Steiner recommended reproducing a text in one's own words in this way to help the participants really unite with the content.

I have found that this also creates a comprehensive view that continues on in the background in later parts of the process when details are worked on and digested.

In the *second step* I then ask the participants to write down what has impressed or moved each one the most. Often they mention specific passages or images, or something about how I expressed a passage in the way I read it aloud, for example with a special sound or gesture. I note down in detail all the points brought up by the participants, and if the group is a large one I try to summarize them in order to find what they have in common or where the emphasis lies.

Frequently the transition from the second to the third step takes place almost immediately. I have to be very alert to this moment since it marks the point when I have to select a few of the items expressed in the 'relating' process so that I can lead them across into the 'digesting' process. This item or these items then provide the focus for several further sessions or lessons with the group.

In the *third step* (digesting) I generally get the participants to practise a number of breathing and speech exercises to prepare their speech instrument for the task of artistically digesting the content. I then take the item or items selected in the second step in order to carry them across into the digesting process. For example we might work on the item by means of speech sounds in exercises that deepen the relevant consonants and vowels. We search together for the main gestures in the item. Or we express the item by means of drama, shaping the various characters and events. First I explain how this might be done and then we put it into practice together. I correct the participants' artistic expression if it does not correspond to the content.

I had an especially gratifying experience during a recent course when we were trying to express in drama one of the passages we had selected during the relating (warming) stage. Almost all the participants were actively involved in an intense debate about which soul-nuances were correct for each of the figures. Looking around me I noticed to my delight that we were now 'well and truly into digesting'.

I have so far only reached the *fourth step* in a few courses. At the end of the digesting step we come together once more while each individual considers what new discoveries he or she has made. We tell each other about them and I help, or we help one another, to identify them better. Then I lead the participants on to the *fifth step*. I describe how one can go even more deeply into the item or items if one can find a suitable exercise which can then lead on to acquiring a new capability.

At this point a number of participants have felt joyful because they had the feeling: 'Now I have something concrete that I can take home with me from this course, something that I can continue to work on in practice.'

This is as far as I have progressed to date. My impression is that it makes quite a difference to the participants whether I work out the entire course in advance or whether we construct the content together out of a mutual warming process (second step). By this latter means the course develops into each individual's own way of working artistically on his or her own personal theme. In addition new depths are reached in what goes on during the course. A learning community comes into being which provides considerable support for individuals in overcoming their own learning blockages.

6. Destiny Learning in Organizations
by Lauri Salonen

Destiny (or karma) means different things to different people. Some are fatalistic about it, while others see it in terms of 'blows of fate'. For me it is like a manuscript for the book of my life, and even as it approaches inexorably it leaves a great deal of room for manoeuvre. Above all it is a stimulus to develop and an opportunity to learn.

Destiny played a decisive role in my choice of profession. Having embarked on a scientific career, I called in at my laboratory during my period of military service for a consultation about the next stage of my research project. Once there I happened to pick up a scientific report that began with exactly the same words as a paper I had published some time ago. This experience raised doubts in my mind as to whether I should continue working at that establishment, doubts that gradually led me to question whether I wanted to follow a scientific career at all. Then I woke up one morning with a sure feeling that I would leave the lab and begin to work with people. This is the path I am still following today in my work as an adult educator and management consultant in Finland and many other countries.

Management consultant and Destiny Learning

Having worked with Destiny Learning and its seven steps for a number of years, and having organized several seminars in Finland and practised in our small group of consultants, I offered my colleagues in the Innotiimi Group the opportunity to work on destiny questions in the autumn of 1997. This was the first seminar in this field in the Finnish language. None of the participants had a background in anthroposophy.

Innotiimi is a group of about 25 management consultants with whom I work regularly. Its members frequently undertake further development and they are open to new methods and in some cases also to spiritual ideas. I had already worked with them, for example for a whole year on the spiritual background to the work of the consultant. Having told them I would be willing to go in more depth into Destiny Learning, I described the method briefly. I did not canvass anyone and of course participation was entirely voluntary.

Of the 12 who had enrolled, nine attended. In advance of the weekend I had made it clear that the method would be a conscious learning process, that there was no need to have any specific beliefs, and that those who did not want to continue on this path after the end of the seminar could then consider the matter closed. The one condition was that the reality of reincarnation must be accepted as a working hypothesis and that during the seminar there would be no discussion about whether it was a fact or not.

We began on Friday evening, on the Saturday work continued until late, and the seminar ended on Sunday afternoon. We worked in two groups, except for the very beginning when we introduced ourselves to one another, each stating what 'destiny' meant to him or her. This proved to be such a lively introduction to the subject that later seminars came to be opened in the same way.

In my introductory talk I again emphasized the one condition of accepting reincarnation as a hypothesis for the duration of the weekend. On the other hand I encouraged the participants to give free reign to their questions and doubts. I described how destiny is seen in other cultures and religions, and this provided the backdrop for our specific project: to learn consciously from everyday life, in other words from destiny.

The seven steps of Destiny Learning were described in brief, and each person then began with some minor everyday event. In the next step we looked for similar events in our lives. They might have been quite different, or even mirror images of the first event, but the aim was to find what had been similar in the way we responded. In the third step we felt our way towards possible causes lying in the past which might be the reason why we always respond in a similar way to certain situations. In the fourth step we began to make the acquaintance of this being within us that reacts in this way.

The seminar ended with Step Five, in which the participants formulated a preliminary plan for remaining in conversation with that newly-discovered shadow being. Why do we keep on coming up against similar situations? What are our reactions trying to tell us? What should we be learning from them?

The seven steps have been described at length in the present book. The aim of my introduction was to make them generally comprehensible in a humorous way while avoiding specialist terminology.

Most of the time we worked in the smaller groups, with my introductions to the combined group taking the form of quite brief sketches. 'Theoretical explanations' came later, after the work in the smaller groups, depending on what questions were asked. No long lectures were given, the process being one of 'learning through doing'. This way of working has proved the most useful in what we do here.

Once or twice we also resorted to drawing. First we drew the 'essence' of the initial event, and then in Step Four the 'other being' and its metamorphosis.

The consultants on the course had experiences similar to those in other seminars. Some gained a very clear picture of the past. When this happens the former incarnation shines through into the present personality so strongly that gestures, movements, the manner of speaking and indeed a person's whole being suddenly change. People are tremendously relieved at being able to grasp the past source of their present motivation. One participant spoke of having tried to work on a specific problem for years only to find it slipping from his grasp again and again like a piece of soap. This seminar had at last enabled him to get a proper grip on it.

With these management consultants I also tried to find a new way in which each could continue to work alone after the end of the seminar. The group worked together on feeling their way towards various possibilities. I had not done anything quite like this before, but these colleagues were already accustomed to working very intensely with each other's inmost questions.

What did I myself gain from this seminar? First of all I was pleased to have helped the participants progress a little way along their own path. Several of them had stated initially that they felt very inadequate in many ways and had so much that needed to be improved or even healed. Our systematic method helped them become better at observing their own shadow side and at making a plan of how to continue living with it. Even when, as in this case, there is not much time, the process always concludes with a plan for continuing to practise in everyday life.

I believe that this process of Destiny Learning can help every consultant or adviser improve his professional work. When you work on events in your own life you also get better at noticing the destiny forces at work in social situations. In management consultancy it is especially important to have at least some insight into the destiny web of those involved, for this enables you to see more clearly what can help the specific organization in tackling its problems. The ability to perceive the forces of destiny is a capability that will be essential for the management consultant.

Organizations learn from destiny

My second example is a seminar held in Holland early in 1998 in collaboration with colleagues of the Dutch management consultancy group NPI. The purpose was to test a new kind of Destiny Learning in answer to the question: 'How can employees—in this case managers—find that element in their destiny which links them with their particular organization?' This is of course intimately bound up with people's career, or rather with their personal path in professional life: 'What has one's professional path got to do with one's specific job?'

Another important point in this seminar was the idea that organizations, too, have their own shadow side, their own 'double'. The employees' personal 'doubles' work together in an organization, thus creating a kind of 'organization double'.

The marked and important difference between this and earlier seminars was that in this case the destiny event worked on in Step One had to be something that had happened in the participant's professional life.

Step Two involved finding other events of a similar quality also in participants' professional lives. If Step One had gone well, as in the group I was leading, it proved surprisingly easy to discover the same gesture in other events along people's professional path. This was perhaps helped by the fact that time was rather short.

Many of the managers said that the seminar had helped them find the thread of continuity running through their own lives, and once you understand your own path you can also gain a better understanding of the situation at your place of work. It is like opening a window through which to look from a new angle not only at the organization's conflict situations and other critical points but also possible solutions to these problems. The reasons for a good many difficult situations at work are not necessarily as rational as might be expected.

Summary

Having progressed through the seven processes in the right way we find it much easier to discern the forces of destiny wherever we look. By 'forces of destiny' I mean everything that began in earlier lives and now causes people to respond to events in a deadlocked fashion. Rational thought alone cannot solve difficult situations, and so a new kind of management is called for, management based on the ability to perceive the forces of destiny.

The starting-point of a new way of working both for consultants and managers is the ability to perceive accurately the situation in one's own organization. The whole methodology of Destiny Learning is based on accurate perceptions. This provides the basis on which one can practise the ability to discern destiny at work in everyday life. Another important aspect of this whole method is that destiny is taken to be an everyday matter rather than something mystical or distant. So it can be talked about in perfectly normal, everyday language.

Increasingly reincarnation and karma are subjects discussed by the media, but in such a mixed up manner that they cannot be taken seriously. My seminars on Destiny Learning with management consultants and managers have shown clearly that these subjects can be dealt with in a way that does not put people off. Working with the seven steps of Destiny Learning using normal language is perfectly acceptable as one way of working in business life.

It is not a matter of wanting to 'sell' the idea of reincarnation. A seminar plunges right in with actual exercises. The only condition is that reincarnation is accepted as a working hypothesis and therefore not discussed during the seminar. Participants must be willing to enter a process and see what comes of it in the end. The steps of the process follow one another in a natural sequence. The course facilitator should always take care not to put his own interpretation on things or make decisions on behalf of the participants.

I have tried out this method so often that I have every confidence in its effectiveness and integrity. In future I want to develop Destiny Learning further, specifically in connection with organizations, although I do not yet know exactly how this will turn out. The aim, of course, will be to help organizations tackle the next phases in their development. Motivation is often one of the problems, for any development calls for motivation. Destiny Learning is one way of helping people to be better motivated. Over and above this it is also an excellent way of finding one's own shadow and the shadow of one's organization.

We have brought our own shadow, our 'double', into being by our own past actions. It follows us everywhere. It is because of this shadow that we often behave in ways we ourselves regard as negative, and this is why it is so difficult to look this shadow steadily in the eye and accept it. Sometimes we are totally incapable of taking a decision, or we turn our

Destiny Learning in Organizations 215

back on a situation at the very moment when we ought to do something about it. It is extremely annoying to stand in one's own way like this! Destiny Learning transforms our shadow, which we first took to be something entirely negative, into our best friend and teacher. But before we can make friends with it we have to see and accept it.

It is important for all of us to accept our own shadow side, but it is especially important for those who occupy positions of leadership, for such people are often rather isolated. Their 'double' is all too visible to others while they themselves fail to notice it at all. When such a person comes face to face with his shadow it can be a very depressing experience if he cannot bring himself to broach the matter with any of his colleagues.

Some management consultants are all too aware of their own shadow. On the other hand there is always a danger of the consultant's shadow getting into conversation with the client's shadow. Consultants must try everything out on themselves and use themselves as an instrument. Then their own efforts with their own shadow will help them in their work with clients and their problems.

In my experience Destiny Learning works best with people who are not too familiar with anthroposophy or some similar world view because the initial stages are then less weighed down by ready-made concepts. The greatest difficulties arise with those who have consulted a 'clairvoyant' and therefore already 'know' it all. It is a real battle to forget the images provided by the clairvoyant and step out along the learning path instead.

If you refrain from trying to influence people's opinions they are usually ready and open to working with destiny. For me the real challenge is to develop a method of working with the seven steps in professional life in a way that makes it unnecessary to use the word 'reincarnation' at all. I am sure it is possible to help people gain an awareness of the intersecting threads present in any place of work without having to offer them a theoretical or philosophical introduction. Once this has been achieved it will be possible to help every individual and every organization. Questions about reincarnation and karma should only arise subsequently, once people have become familiar with the subject through their own activities and experiences gained in practising with the forces of destiny.

*

Finally I want to thank two of my consultant colleagues for their help in preparing this article. Adriaan Bekman of the NPI interviewed me initially. Päivi Suokas of the Finnish Biodynamic Association then reworked the interview to form a coherent text.

7. How Biography Work Relates to Destiny Learning
by Karl Heinz Finke

Towards the end of our first seminar on 'Learning from Destiny in Seven Steps' at Berlin's Forum Kreuzberg, Coenraad van Houten asked the participants: 'Does Destiny Learning on its own provide access to a deeper understanding of one's circumstances in life and one's biography, or should one first work through one's biography systematically with the help of biography counselling?' This was not meant as a request for information that could be answered immediately. It was a research question to which we have returned repeatedly during the course of many foundation and follow-up seminars. As a lecturer, a group facilitator in seminars, and as a biography counsellor, I use both methods. The approach I choose develops out of the initial situation and the way questions are asked.

The research question

Here are some preliminary answers to the above research question as to whether it is fruitful for Destiny Learning to be preceded by biography work.

Having carried out and thoroughly evaluated a number of seminars we have reached the conclusion that Destiny Learning can be successful without being preceded by biography work. Many participants have attended our seminars knowing nothing at all about biography work, and they have had no special difficulty in following the lectures or participating in the group work.

One blockage regularly encountered by participants taking part for the first time in the Destiny Learning process is finding a suitable 'event' to describe in the group work. Although it is a question of selecting an experience that one can remember well and describe objectively, any biography work one might have done is no help in this respect. The problems involved in choosing a suitable event arise because the subject 'destiny' tempts people to bring up something too elaborate. The word 'destiny' reminds them of weighty existential problems and tempts them to forget that destiny has just as much of a hand in everyday irritations as well.

I had expected that prior biography work would have a positive effect in Step Two (uniting the destiny event with one's biography). In this step the participant in question has to find further biographical events with similar qualities. The gesture that has emerged from the first event becomes a window through which one can survey the whole of life's landscape. Practice has shown that prior biography work provides no particular help in this. Describing an event awakens in the participant a feeling for its gesture and qualities, and once this has happened a whole fountain of other biographical memories floods out. One participant in the group work was heard to say: 'Well, if that is the case it applies to the whole of my life!'

On the other hand there is a blockage that comes up especially in participants who have taken part in biography work. They tend to choose an event in Step One on the premise that they are already aware of similar events in their biography. Since they think they already know something, some of the open-mindedness they need for the process is lost. In some cases the whole report they give to the group is coloured by what they assume the connections to be. If this turns out to be beside the point, the group has to help them chisel away a lot of residue in order to get at the core of the event. I have also found that misinterpretations of biographical events reached in other seminars or in individual work can also lead to this situation. It is more difficult to sweep aside an error than it is to find new ways towards understanding a problem.

Collaboration between Destiny Learning and biography work

Having gone through the Destiny Learning process several times, I began to adapt my way of working in biography groups and individual biography conversations. Now (January 1998) I have developed various ways of working, some of which are a mixture of biography work and Destiny Learning. The approach I choose arises out of the initial situation or the questions that are asked.

The point of departure for a biography seminar

I apply biography work in order to help the participants reach a conscious overview of their own life and circumstances. Progress is achieved by focussing on key questions and key years which I suggest and on key events which the participants select. They can thus survey their biography and gain an inkling of the line of continuity running through it like Ariadne's thread. Destiny Learning is then applied to stimulate and strengthen their ability to recognize lifelong themes, crisis points, decision points, repetitions or metamorphoses. Attention is drawn to these points by questions or remarks. The process of 'finding the thread of continuity' highlights specific facts as being especially important, problematical, symptomatic and so on. Destiny Learning then enables the participant to take a closer look at these core points.

To compare the two, I could say that I use biography work as a telescope and Destiny Learning as a microscope. If the subjects rising to the surface appear to be very intimate or bound up with very strong feelings I also offer the participant in question some individual conversation sessions concurrently or after the seminar or group work. I hope it is not presumptuous to say that I feel my ability to detect such points has been strengthened through my own work with Destiny Learning.

Biography and karma

People decide to embark on biography work or Destiny Learning for all kinds of reasons. They may be concerned with a specific event or question, or they may be searching in a more generalized way: 'I feel pushed around by life; such a lot is expected of me but I can't seem to find any rhyme or reason to it all.'

Where there are specific events or questions it is helpful to use Steps I and II of Destiny Learning as a microscope. Through these you can obtain a factual and qualitative picture of the problem and its immediate biographical implications. I point out that the obstacles we encounter today might originate in a former life; but it is up to the enquirer to decide whether he or she wants to enter into that dimension. You usually only need a few sessions (about three) to reach the point where the enquirer will signal: 'This is fine; I can find my own way from here.' Colleagues have told me that this method can also help unravel human relationships and partnership problems quickly and effectively.

When the questions are more general I try to help enquirers attain an overall view of their life by asking key questions, finding out about experiences at the ego-points in their biography, and by asking about on-going themes (repetitions) and key experiences.

Precisely when a question is rather general, however, it can also be very helpful to bring out a few events in much more detail by means of the steps in Destiny Learning. Biography work is a good preliminary to Steps I and II. It is up to the enquirers to decide how far they want to go. Many do want to go further as they begin to see their life from an entirely new perspective. Concentrating on specific points then helps them develop new ways of proceeding or practising.

The original purpose of biography work

Bernard Lievegoed published *De levensloop van de mens*[3] in Holland in 1976. With this book he launched biography work on the basis of anthroposophy. Unfortunately I never met him, but former colleagues of his have told me that he wanted biography work to be a door through which people might approach reincarnation and karma, subjects which, at that time, could not easily be broached in public.

In the seminars, discussion groups and individual conversations I work with, it has meanwhile become quite rare for someone to have scruples about including reincarnation and karma among the thoughts brought forward to elaborate on a theme, and such people are usually quite satisfied by my suggestion to follow the example set by scientists when they posit a working hypothesis. Hardly ever have I experienced total rejection of these ideas, for example on the basis of a fundamentalist Christian view or a strictly scientific outlook. I can talk about this subject quite openly with most people and often find that they have already gone into it quite thoroughly, developing their own ideas and questions about it. The plethora of publications on it in recent years would seem to demonstrate that reincarnation and karma are the 'talk of the town'. The tactful reticence on the part of anthroposophists with regard to mentioning this subject now appears to me to be quaintly old-fashioned.

Intensive preoccupation with our own biography and those of others leads us with an inexorable inner logic to ask where we come from and where we are going. On the other hand it is also possible to become so engrossed in examining, mirroring and tracing connections within a single biography that one no longer includes reincarnation and karma in one's considerations, thus getting stuck within a single life while the doors leading to 'before' and 'after' remain firmly closed. It is my experience that this can happen both in individual work with biography counsellors and in groups led by a facilitator. It is an easy trap to fall into, for there is such an abundance of interesting material to fascinate us.

In the way I work I endeavour to help modern individuals, who are at home in western culture, experience how reincarnation and karma are linked both with the concept of development and with the Christ-impulse.

Final Comment and Summary

In my Foreword I stated that this whole book rests on the question of what capabilities adult human beings will need today and in the future in order to cope with the new situation the world finds itself in. Some characteristics of this new situation are as follows:

1. Today's world is largely interdependent, so we must learn to understand the global dynamic processes and learn to think and act in accordance with them.
2. We now have a global economy.
3. Technological progress is rapid and is fast making it possible to control everything.
4. Various forces are working towards achieving a political world order that will only function under some form of central control.
5. The type of human being who acts and functions in an orderly fashion and adapts sensibly to it, while remaining happy and contented, is on the way to becoming the ideal in the new world order.

Would such a human being still be human?

The reader of my earlier book[1] as well as the present one will by now have realized that everything both books stand for pursues a fundamentally different path. The new capabilities described in connection with the seven professional fields aim to help human beings actively learn from the above-listed facts and trends so that cultural progress can nevertheless take place in the midst of those new circumstances. This must happen in every realm—in economic life, in socio-political life and especially in an independent cultural life. Actually an independent cultural life hardly exists as yet, since almost all educational establishments and training models make use of educational modules and methods that render learning controllable. This is especially true in cases where they are dependent on politics and/or economics and thus not independent. Such establishments are like strongholds of those endeavours that are trying to create a standard and suitably conditioned human being.

Of course there are also exceptions where courageous individuals, in the face of every constraint imposed by the system, are striving to awaken the living human spirit. Against this background let us look once more at the seven professional fields and the two fundamental principles.

If all education and training could be imbued in endeavours to awaken the will and cultivate the sense of truth, this would contribute a great deal towards building up a many-layered and highly diverse cultural life while at the same time countering those forms of conditioning that are striving to establish a standardized world order. The sense of truth involves a conscious search for truth. It comes into being when our spirit seeks for the truth. It appears as a higher consciousness and can sometimes be experienced as light. When the will is awakened the voice of conscience appears out of the dark unconscious like an all-consuming flame alongside the sense of truth. Novalis wrote: 'By grasping conscience we bring it into being.' This could be the adult educator's motto, for it is also true to say of the sense of truth: 'By wanting the sense of truth we bring it into being.'

*

If in your teaching you succeed in relating selfless observation (Professional Field I) with independent judgement-forming (Professional Field II) in such a way that an 'open space in between' is created, then you will have overcome the compelling short-circuit that can arise between sensual stimulus and instinctive judgement forming. Out of an open space in the middle a free space is born. The formation of such an open middle in the human being is linked with the heritage of European cultural life, for it is in the spiritual life of culture that a new open space can come into being between East and West, and a new bridge be built between the cultures of the Germanic and the Slavonic peoples.

Europe's task was well and truly destroyed during the

twentieth century. Now, instead of achieving its aims, Europe is rather helplessly embroiled in the effort to achieve political unity while at the same time being determined by global economic interests. What happens in the future will depend on whether we (and generations to come) will succeed in exchanging external standardization for a 'unity in diversity' by enabling the individual human spirit to unfold.

To 'individualize' what we have learnt is in every field the heart and core of the adult learning process, whether it be Vocational Learning, Destiny Learning (self-knowledge) or Spiritual Research Learning.

Between the lines of what has been set down in this book the reader will everywhere discern ideas that have lived as ideals in the best spirits of Europe and also North America (Emerson, for example). The seeds sown by European idealism are now Europe's heritage, a heritage which, although still dormant at present, is endowed with spiritual life forces of such strength that it could be transformed into an adult education suitable for the present time. An adult education of this calibre is now, though, no longer only Europe's affair, for it concerns the world as a whole. The author knows from experience that a renewal of adult education is as necessary in North America, Malaysia, Australia, New Zealand, South Africa, and so on, as it is in Europe.

So what happens when the two professional fields, 'the ability to encounter others' (III) and 'the three learning paths' (IV), are brought together in harmony?

The 'open space in the middle' is nourished by real encounter and is realized by threefold learning. This involves a relationship between something that unites and something that is active individually, between something social and something solitary, something essentially feminine and something essentially masculine. When these two elements are joined together a third element can be born and begin to develop. Biologically it is one of the great miracles that a man and a woman can bring about fertilization that allows an 'individual' child to enter the world. These two realms are also spiritually present in every human being.

Final Comment and Summary 225

Geographically, Europe is a meeting place of two realms—the eastern and the western. The wall erected down the middle of Europe was a physical sign showing that 'never the twain would meet' during the twentieth century. Slav culture was all but devoured by communism while the European-Germanic culture came to be subsumed by western economic principles (the 'economic miracle'). A breathing 'open space' between East and West was unable to unfold, so Europe lost its soul. This is not the place to discuss the political and economic situation in detail, but it is very much to the point to describe how it relates to adult education. The nations of Europe are for the most part now fully adapted to the western powers who are seeking to establish a centralized world leadership and world order in which there would be no place for an individual European identity to mediate between East and West.

From Thomas Meyer's biography of Ludwig Polzer-Hoditz,[2] especially the chapter about the testament of Peter the Great, we adult educators can gain at least an inkling of why a renewal of adult education is so important now.

Polzer-Hoditz considered it to be the task of the European nations, including the British, to meet the economic power streaming eastwards from the West and transcend its principles and methods, thus bringing into being something that the East, right up to Asia, would be able to absorb fruitfully. And vice versa, everything streaming westwards from the East must be transformed in the European sphere into something that will become spiritually fruitful for the West.

It is in Europe that the encounter, the bridge, indeed the marriage between Slav culture and western European culture should take place so that from this open space in the middle something new can be born that can transform, heal and harmonize the global East-West confrontation.

Obviously an independent cultural, spiritual life such as can arise through the three learning paths must be an essential ingredient in this. If Europe fails in the coming century to exercise this harmonizing, balancing and peace-making function, the consequence will be a battle for the leadership of humanity between Asia (China?) and the West (the USA?) that will devastate the world.

Finally let us turn to day-time and night-time learning (Professional Fields V and VI) about which we have already said a good deal. What we practise and strive for during the day makes it possible for learning to take place during the night, which means that something speaks to us spiritually during our night-time consciousness. And what speaks to us spiritually during the night works on into our day-time consciousness. We need these two both for our earthly and our spiritual life.

All this should render the form of the seven Professional Fields as depicted in Diagram 3 even more alive and meaningful.

The seven learning processes as the source and foundation stone of adult learning have been described in detail above. To draw attention to the connection between future adult learning and the situation in which both Europe and the world find themselves may show how urgently we need a new adult learning that can meet the challenge of our time.

Notes

Foreword and Introduction (pages 1–9)

1. C. van Houten, *Awakening the Will. Principles and Processes in Adult Learning*, Temple Lodge Publishing, London 1999. Original German *Erwachsenenbildung als Willenserweckung*, Verlag Freies Geistesleben, Stuttgart 1993.
2. Ibid.

Part One (pages 13–62)

1. C. van Houten, *Awakening the Will*, op. cit.
2. György Konrad, *Antipolitik*, Frankfurt am Main 1984.
3. Friedrich Schiller, *On the Aesthetic Education of Man*, translated and with an Introduction by R. Snell, Fred. Ungar Publishing Co., New York 1965. This quotation translated by C. van Houten.
4. Further works relevant to this section are: F. W. Zeylmans van Emmichoven, *The Anthroposophical Understanding of the Soul*, Anthroposophic Press, Spring Valley 1982; R. Steiner, *A Theory of Knowledge Implicit in Goethe's World Conception* (GA 2), Anthroposophic Press, New York 1978.
5. Stefan Leber, *Der Schlaf und seine Bedeutung*, Stuttgart 1996.
6. Further helpful reading relevant to this chapter: R. Steiner, *Die menschliche Seele in ihrem Zusammenhang mit göttlich-geistigen Individualitäten* (GA 224), Dornach 1992, lecture of 2 May 1923.

Part Two (pages 65–137)

1. R. Steiner, *Reincarnation and Karma* (GA 135), Anthroposophic Press, New York 1992. See also R. Steiner, *Theosophy* (GA 9), Anthroposophic Press, New York 1994.
2. R. Steiner, *Karmic Relationships, Vol. 2* (GA 236), Rudolf Steiner Press, London 1974, lecture of 4 May 1924.

3 R. Steiner *Karmic Relationships, Vols I—VIII* (GA 235-240), Rudolf Steiner Press, London, various dates.
4 R. Steiner, *Karmic Relationships, Vol 2*, op. cit., lecture of 9 May 1924.
5 Also helpful in Learning Step III: N. Rohlfs, 'Wie stellen wir die Frage nach dem Karma?' in *Mitteilungen aus der anthroposophischen Arbeit in Deutschland*, Easter I/1998, No. 203.
6 G. Kienle, *Christentum und Medizin*, Stuttgart 1986, fourth lecture.
7 See also S. Leber, *Der Schlaf und seine Bedeutung*, op. cit.
8 P. Archiati, *Reincarnation in Modern Life*, Temple Lodge Publishing, London 1997, fourth lecture.
9 Regarding Learning Step V see also: R. Steiner, *Overcoming Nervousness* (in GA 143), Anthroposophic Press, New York 1978; and *Reincarnation and Karma*, op. cit. Also S. Leber, *Der Schlaf und seine Bedeutung*, op. cit.
10 See C. Van Houten, *Awakening the Will*, op. cit.
11 G. Kienle, *Christentum und Medizin*, op. cit., p.47.
12 Also helpful in Learning Step VII: R. Steiner, *From Jesus to Christ*, (GA 131), Rudolf Steiner Press, Sussex 1991; and *Karmic Relationships, Vols I-VIII*, op. cit.
13 J. E. Zeylmans van Emmichoven, *Who was Ita Wegman? A Documentation, Vol.I 1876-1925*, Mercury Press, Spring Valley 1995.
14 Also helpful for Steps VI and VII and the final chapters: R. Steiner, *The Philosophy of Spiritual Activity, a Philosophy of Freedom*, Rudolf Steiner Press, Bristol 1992; and C. van Houten, *Awakening the Will*, op. cit.

Part Three (pages 141–168)

1 P. T. Hugenholz, *Over tijd en tijdsvormen*, Zutphen 1938.
2 F. W. Zeylmans van Emmichoven, *The Anthroposophical Understanding of the Soul*, op. cit.
3 S. Leber, *Der Schlaf und seine Bedeutung*, op. cit.

Part Four (pages 171–221)

1 For further information on seminars and publications on Dynamic Judgement Forming please apply to Foundation

Dialogue, Weegbreeplantsoen 21, NL-2651 MA Berkel en Rodenrys, Holland.
2 R. Steiner *Speech and Drama* (GA 282), Anthroposophic Press, New York & Rudolf Steiner Press, London 1986.
3 B. Lievegoed *Phases, The Spiritual Rhythms in Adult Life*, Rudolf Steiner Press, London 1997.

Final Comment and Summary (pages 222–226)

1 C. van Houten, *Awakening the Will*, op. cit.
2 T. Meyer, *Ludwig Polzer-Hoditz. Ein Europäer*, Perseus Verlag, Basle 1994, especially the chapters 'Das Testament Peters des Grossen', and 'Ausblick in das 21. Jahrhundert'.

Awakening the Will
Principles and Processes in Adult Learning
Coenraad van Houten

How do adults learn? What is the task of the adult educator in adult education? What can adults do to take charge of their learning process?

Learning means change and transformation. But in order to learn, argues Coenraad van Houten, we must first awaken our will. True adult education, he says, enables our spiritual ego to accomplish this. He describes the forms in which learning can be meaningfully structured, and offers advice and ideas to help overcome specific learning blockages.

This book regards the business of adult education as a full profession, and it provides a theoretical and practical basis for its true task: an awakening of the will.

192pp; ISBN 1 902636 11 2; £11.95

A note from the publisher

For more than a quarter of a century, **Temple Lodge Publishing** has made available new thought, ideas and research in the field of spiritual science.

Anthroposophy, as founded by Rudolf Steiner (1861-1925), is commonly known today through its practical applications, principally in education (Steiner-Waldorf schools) and agriculture (biodynamic food and wine). But behind this outer activity stands the core discipline of spiritual science, which continues to be developed and updated. True science can never be static and anthroposophy is living knowledge.

Our list features some of the best contemporary spiritual-scientific work available today, as well as introductory titles. So, visit us online at **www.templelodge.com** and join our emailing list for news on new titles.

If you feel like supporting our work, you can do so by buying our books or making a direct donation (we are a non-profit/ charitable organisation).

office@templelodge.com

TEMPLE LODGE
For the finest books of Science and Spirit